Soundings

Issue 16
Civil
Society

EDITORS
Stuart Hall
Doreen Massey
Michael Rustin

GUEST EDITOR
Andreas Hess

POETRY EDITOR
Carole Satyamurti

REVIEWS EDITORS
Becky Hall and
Susanna Rustin

ART EDITOR
Tim Davison

EDITORIAL OFFICE
Lawrence & Wishart
99a Wallis Road
London E9 5LN

Soundings is published three
times a year, in autumn,
spring and summer by:
Soundings Ltd
c/o **Lawrence & Wishart**
99a Wallis Road
London E9 5LN
Email: soundings@l-w-bks.demon.co.uk
Website: www.l-w-bks.co.uk/sounding.html

ADVERTISEMENTS
Write for information to Soundings,
c/o Lawrence & Wishart

SUBSCRIPTIONS
2001 subscription rates are (for three issues):
UK: Institutions £70, Individuals £35
Rest of the world: Institutions £80, Individuals
£45

Collection as a whole © Soundings 2000
Individual articles © the authors 2000

No article may be reproduced or transmitted by any
means, electronic or mechanical, including
photocopying, recording or any information storage
and retrieval system, without the permission in writing
of the publisher, editor or author

ISSN 1362 6620
ISBN 0 85315 929 7

Text setting Art Services, Norwich
Cover photograph: © Grazyna Kubica-Heller

Printed in Great Britain by
Cambridge University Press, Cambridge

CONTENTS

──────────────── *Continued on next page* ────────────────

Continued from previous page

NOTES ON CONTRIBUTORS

Jeffrey C. Alexander is Professor of Sociology at the University of California, Los Angeles. He is the author, editor and co-editor of several books including *Real Civil Societies* (Sage 1998), *Neofunctionalism and After* (Blackwell 1998) and *Diversity and Its Discontents* (Princeton University Press 1999).

Paul Allen teaches creative writing at the College of Charleston in South Carolina. His second poetry collection, *The Clean Plate Club*, will be published by Salmon Press next year.

Andrew Blake is Professor and Head of Cultural Studies at King Alfred's College, Winchester.

Catherine Byron teaches writing and medieval literature at Nottingham Trent University. Her fifth collection of poems, *The Getting of Vellum*, appears later this year.

Susie Campbell teaches English in a London comprehensive school and runs a new writing theatre company.

Rosalind Delmar is a counsellor, writer and translator.

Robert Fine is Reader at the University of Warwick. He is the editor and co-editor of *Civil Society* (Frank Cass Publications 1997) and *People, Nation and State* (I. B. Tauris 1999).

Jonathan Freedland is a columnist for *The Guardian*. He is also the author of *Bring Home the Revolution - The Case for a British Republic* (Fourth Estate 1998).

Paulette Goudge is a freelance trainer and consultant in equal opportunities and development issues. She is currently completing her PhD on whiteness and power.

G. C. Harcourt is Emeritus Reader in the History of Economic Theory, Cambridge University, Emeritus Fellow, Jesus College, Cambridge and Professor Emeritus, University of Adelaide (1988). He has been a member of the Australian Labor Party since 1954. He is a most inactive member of the Market Ward of the British Labour Party in Cambridge. He votes in the UK and Oz.

Jonathan Hearn is a cultural anthropologist and Lecturer in Politics and Sociology at the University of Edinburgh.

Andreas Hess is Lecturer in Sociology at the University of Wales, Bangor and author of *American Social and Political Thought, 2000*.

Grazyna Kubica-Heller is a social anthropologist at Jagiellonian University Krakow. She is co-editor of *Malinowski, Between Two Worlds* (Cambridge University Press 1988).

María Pía Lara is Professor of Philosophy at Universidad Autonoma Metropolitana, Mexico City, and author of *Moral Textures - Feminist Narratives in the Public Sphere* (University of California Press 1998).

Michael Laskey is the founder of the Aldeburgh Poetry Festival, and co-editor of the magazine *Smith's Knoll*. His latest collection of poetry is *The Tightrope Wedding*.

Simon Lewis teaches African literature at the College of Charleston, South Carolina, and edits the little literary magazine *Illuminations*. His work is chiefly concerned with the representation of landscape in colonial and postcolonial African literature.

William Outhwaite is Professor of Sociology at the University of Sussex. He is the author of *Habermas: A Critical Introduction* (Polity 1994) and editor of *The Habermas Reader* (Polity 1996).

Emma Satyamurti is a trainee solicitor in a London legal practice

Claire Wallace is a professor and researcher at the Institute for Advanced Studies in Vienna. Her most recent publications are: *Youth in Society. The construction and deconstruction of youth in East and West Europe* (with Siyaka Kovacheva, Macmillan 1998) and *Central Europe: New Migration* (with Dariusz Stola, Macmillan, forthcoming).

Tom Wengraf is Senior Lecturer in Sociology at Middlesex University. Author of *Qualitative Research Interviewing: semi-structured, biographic and narrative methods*, to be published by Sage in March 2001, he also co-edited *The Turn to Biographical Methods in Social Science* (Routledge 2000). He teaches qualitative research methods and in-depth interviewing.

Frances Wilson teaches, writes and paints. Her collection of poetry, *Close to Home*, is published by Rockingham Press.

Correction

In the last issue we announced that Dan Diner's book *Das Jahrhundert Verstehen* (*Understanding the Century*), which was reviewed by Andreas Hess, was to be published by Polity. Unfortunately this information was incorrect. There is as yet no English language publisher for this book. We apologise for any inconvenience caused by our announcement.

The return of the political repressed

As we complete this issue, the fuel protest has just been called off, the Government has fallen behind the Conservatives in the polls, petrol queues have re-formed and dispersed in response to rumours, and Gordon Brown has been accused of having lied on the *Today* programme. It is a fast-moving situation, and by the time *Soundings 16*, is published, much else will no doubt have happened, just as unexpectedly. Even as we write, a missile is reported to have struck the (illuminated) M16 building on the South Bank of the Thames.

It seems above all that politics is back, and in more dynamic and conflictful ways than have been seen for some years. The signs of class struggle, as some might once have called it, are reversed. Instead of the strikes and poll tax revolts of the 1980s, we see the Countryside Alliance and truck drivers mobilising against the government. (The self-employed have been the vanguard of the right before, road hauliers and truck drivers having been instrumental in the downfall of Salvador Allende in Chile.)

Sooner or later, a New Labour government that was attempting to change anything was going to encounter serious resistance, and we had better become prepared for what follows. Although it was easy to criticise New Labour's control-freakery, etc, there was always some comfort in the fact that they, and not Hague's Conservatives, were the ones in control. High fuel taxes had the purposes of energy-saving, and of discouraging the unsustainable growth of car and lorry traffic, as well as of raising taxes while nobody (as it was thought) would notice. It will be a setback to transport and energy policy if governments are now forced to lower the cost of energy to consumers. The assertion of the prime importance of the private car and truck will be an ideological victory to neo-liberalism.

It turns out that some bad early judgements have come back to haunt the government. What matters in the Brown affair is the reminder of the earlier murky dealings with Ecclestone over tobacco advertising in Formula 1 - not whether he misrepresented a conversation he had in the back of a car with Tony Blair. Plainly the Millennium Dome is not all it might have been. The Government, having shelved John Prescott's transport bill for two years, only acquired a transport policy a few months ago, and so far citizens have seen few benefits from it. Refusing to increase progressive taxation meant that regressive taxation - which includes petrol tax - had to be increased. Much more significant than the disruption of petrol supplies is the fact that most of the public say in opinion polls that they support a reduction of tax, and not all of this can be put down to biased questions. Increasing taxes by stealth is all very well, but what happens if some 'stealth taxes' are unpopular, and opposition becomes mobilised against them? Wouldn't it have been better if the taxes had been fully explained and justified in the first place?

Geoff Mulgan and Robin Murray presciently argued in 1993 for a greater measure of 'hypothecation' of taxes, that is for closer linkages between taxes and the expenditures which they fund.[1] They argued this on democratic grounds, and as a way of addressing the political problems of tax-aversion. There were always going to be practical difficulties in hypothecation, but its advocates rightly saw the 'democratic deficit' in current tax policy, and the problems which would probably arise from this. Clearer connections will now have to be spelled out between the transport system the government wants to see, and ways in which revenues are to be raised to fund it.

Soundings has never had any doubt that a government of the left-of-centre is going to be about the balancing of interests and contending social forces. We have supported a greater 'pluralism' in politics (for example, through devolution - the theme of a future issue), and in the London Mayoral Election. The New

1. Geoff Mulgan & Robin Murray, *Reconnecting Taxation*. Demos 1993.

Labour government has hitherto preferred to make its judgements about balance in secret, so to speak, without allowing the inevitable seams, rifts and choices to become too visible. Personal rumour and gossip have been filling the space that should have been taken up by political debate. This crisis may have changed that. In a press conference, Tony Blair talked reflectively about the difficult problems of achieving balance between conflicting interests and opposed points of view, and how absolutely central this task of balance was to government. He was right. This 'balancing' is now surely going to have to be accomplished in a more public way. The government can only make progress on energy and transport, and indeed in other fields, if it learns to make its case, and to involve on its side those who support what it trying to do, but who have hitherto been left to sit and watch. It is because we think there need to be more populated and active political spaces that *Soundings* has supported the Government's constitutional reforms, and wants them to go further. A government that 'listens' will show that it recognises different points of view, whilst not giving into every pressure group that takes it on.

The Government retains many assets. It will soon, for example, be able to remedy its neglect of the old, and demonstrate its continuing commitment to ensuring decent living standards for all. But normal political life has now returned, just when many might have thought it dead for ever; and we had all better be prepared for bumpier rides ahead.

MJR

Borrowing to make others rich

Peter Howells

Peter Howells looks at the effects on the economy - and on economic redistribution - of the increased earning power of assets as compared to working for a living.

The last few years have seen a steady rise in the price of assets (houses and equities in particular) relative to the prices of goods and services. Since official measures of inflation concentrate upon the latter, recent years of 'low' inflation have been very good for wealth-holders, who have seen both their wealth and income from it rise faster than income from employment. The roots of this development can be traced to the financial deregulation of the early 1980s. By encouraging a large increase in borrowing, it created a corresponding increase in money. With stocks of non-money assets relatively fixed, attempts to maintain money's normal portfolio share have inevitably driven asset prices upward, with important distributional consequences.

Does shareholding beat working for a living? Depending on your job, the answer might well be 'yes' in recent years. Economic theory says this should not be possible, but something very strange has been working to upset the conventional relationship between financial markets and the 'real' economy - not just in the last few years, when it has captured the headlines, but for maybe the last twenty years or more.

Capital gains and income

In October 1998, the FTSE-100 index stood at 5063. By December 1999 it had risen to 6,900, a capital gain equivalent to an annualised rate of return of 32 per cent for those holding a portfolio modelled on the FTSE-100. In fact, the gains were even better than that. The FTSE-100 measures only the change in *price* of its component shares. But shareholders also receive dividends. Some indexes - the German DAX-30 is an example - measure the change not just in the price of shares in the index but in the *total value* of a portfolio composed of the 30 shares, including the dividends received. Adding dividend returns to the capital gain represented by the change in the FTSE-100 raises the annualised rate of return to about 34 per cent. Suppose one were earning the average gross salary for 1998 of about £23,000, with accumulated savings equal to twice that amount invested in the 100 largest ('blue chip') UK shares: an annualised return of 34 per cent would suggest that the £46,000 invested would produce a gross gain of only £16,000. But it should also be borne in mind that a general feature of tax systems is that capital gains are taxed more lightly than income from employment. In the UK, the first £7,200 of capital gains are tax free (a saving of £1600 to an average rate taxpayer). Much of the remainder can now be tax-exempted by the appropriate use of PEPs and now ISAs. Comparing the *net* returns for shareholding and working, the comparison becomes a very close run thing.

While such an experience is clearly beyond many households, for reasons of income as well as custom and habit, it is not completely far-fetched. Savings of £46,000 can be accumulated by saving only five per cent of an average income for fifteen years, compounded at eight per cent - a rate which has been easily achievable since the mid-1970s. (During the 1990s average UK households actually saved eight per cent of disposable income, and compounding would have occurred at more than 10 per cent p.a.) The Office for National Statistics figures for 1998 suggest that some 10 per cent of UK households consisting of two adults with one of pensionable age have liquid assets of this magnitude, while 14 per cent have liquid assets exceeding £20,000. With the passing of the first sizeable generation of owner-occupiers able to bequeath serious housing wealth to their children, these figures should rise sharply in the next few years.

Why is this state of affairs peculiar? The answer lies in some (fairly basic) arithmetic. Conventional wisdom has it that the price of any asset is justified by the income payments it generates over a period of time, discounted by a rate of interest which is composed of three elements. The first element is a *real rate* of return, the rate of return which we require, regardless of anything else - inflation, risk, etc - merely to compensate us for the fact that the benefits lie in the future and that we have to wait for them. (This is often said to measure society's rate of 'time preference' - its preference for consuming something now rather than in future - and it is widely thought to be about three per cent p.a. in rich economies). Since prices tend to rise over time, payments received in the future are diminished in their real purchasing power and so the real rate has to be protected by the addition of the second element, an *inflation premium*. Thirdly, all payments received in the future are strictly speaking uncertain, and this uncertainty attracts a further *risk premium*, historically about six per cent for UK equities. If we take the return on UK government bonds to proxy the first two elements (a real return plus inflation allowance) and add six per cent for risk, the total annual return at the moment should be in the region of 11 per cent p.a.

Now let's look at this another way. The total return to holding shares consists of an annual dividend payment (usually paid in two six-monthly instalments). This absolute sum can easily be turned into a dividend yield by dividing by the price that we paid for the shares (let us represent it by D/P). But as we all know (and as the experience recounted above makes clear), this is but a small part of the attraction of shareholdings. The distinctive nature of shareholding is that the dividend payments, being a claim on nominal profits, tend to increase over time, driven by productivity increases and an upward drift in the general price level. If dividend yields are not to rise toward infinity as the years go by, the price of the shares (P in the denominator) must also rise. Using an orthodox valuation model, it is not difficult to show arithmetically that the rate at which a share's price will rise over time *is* the rate at which dividends are growing. Let us call this g. Then if we let k stand for the total return on shares, then the total return can be decomposed into its two elements, dividend yield and capital gain, and represented as follows:

$$k = \frac{D}{P} + g$$

This brings us to the nub of the problem. Share prices have risen much more rapidly than dividends in recent years. Dividend yields have therefore fallen to very low levels, typically less than 1.5 per cent. (Remember the 'dot.coms' that were briefly so popular at the turn of the millennium? They had no profits, no dividends and thus zero dividend yields). With dividend yields approaching zero, those who hold to these traditional methods of valuation are faced with a dilemma. If the total return to share ownership (k) is to follow its long-run historical course (described by a real rate + inflation premium + risk premium), then dividend growth rates (g) must be entering a (higher) historically unprecedented phase in order to compensate. Alternatively, if dividend growth rates are to stay within historical bounds, the total return from shareholding must in future be moving to unprecedentedly (low) levels. Each possibility has its supporters. For example, technology may be raising the trend growth rate of dividends with the result that the balance of equity returns is shifting towards capital gains. Alternatively, investors may have been convinced that future inflation rates really are going to stay lower than in the past and/or that future business cycles are going to be less volatile, leading to a lower equity risk premium and a lower overall return to equity investment. (A radically different possibility, the spectre at the feast which no one likes to mention, is that this level of prices is completely unsustainable and that a major crash will see dividend yields, g and k restored to their long-run levels, in a re-run of the events of 1987.)

These developments have been well-reported in the popular media and in the financial press.[1] Less well-explored, but certainly implicated, are a number of background conditions which have developed out of the financial deregulation of the 1980s.

The boom in asset trading

The most spectacular of these is the dramatic increase in the UK in financial transactions (broadly defined) relative to transactions arising from the production of goods and services. The standard measure of the latter in any economy is gross domestic (sometimes 'national') product. This aggregates the total expenditure on newly produced goods and services in a defined time period, usually one year, and is a measure not just of expenditure but simultaneously of the value of output or production. What other expenditures are there, one might ask? Many, as it turns out. Firstly, the GDP figures count

---

1. For a succinct commentary, see *Bank of England Quarterly Bulletin*, November 1999, pp330-31.

only the value of finished goods and services. Excluded are all the 'intermediate' transactions that firms engage in with their suppliers and sub-contractors. Excluded, too, are all transactions in second-hand goods (most house purchases in the UK, therefore). So too are most financial transactions, since these involve transfers of ownership of existing assets rather than the production of anything. (A stockbroker's commission is included in GDP, since it represents a service provided, but the far larger sum which is paid for the shares transferred is not).

In 'normal' circumstances one might expect the ratio of total transactions to bear some fairly stable multiple relationship to GDP. After all, the number of intermediate transactions which lie behind the manufacture of a Ford Focus depends upon the degree of vertical integration in the motor industry, and this is not likely to change dramatically in any short period of time. Indeed, the possibility that total transactions might diverge from GDP is routinely dismissed in economics textbooks as an uninteresting theoretical possibility. But some earlier economists knew better, especially when it came to the *financial* components of total spending. Irving Fisher (in 1911 and again in 1926) distinguished between GDP transactions and financial transactions - presumably because he thought they might behave independently. Keynes, in the *Treatise on Money* (1930) was much more explicit:

> The pace at which a circle of financiers, speculators and investors, hand round to one another particular pieces of wealth, or title to such, which they are neither producing nor consuming but merely exchanging, bears no definite relation to the rate of current production. The volume of such transactions is subject to very wide and incalculable fluctuations.

For many years, total transactions in the UK exceeded GDP transactions by a multiple of approximately 25 to one. During the 1980s, this multiple shot up to about 45. Why should this have been?

There are a few clues in the figures which come from the Association for Payment Clearing Systems (APACS). APACS monitors and records the transactions which pass through the three UK clearing companies. (Aggregating them actually understates the true magnitude of total transactions, since the data exclude transactions in notes and coin, and between customers of the same bank branch by cheque - since these do not go through the clearing process). Of the three clearing companies, CHAPS (the Clearing House Automated Payments System) dominates by value. In 1994, CHAPS processed £26 'million-million'-worth of transactions, while the other two systems processed approximately £2 'million-million'-worth. CHAPS is almost uniquely a system for 'wholesale' payments. Unlike the retail systems where clearing takes several days, payments via CHAPS are available on the day that they are made. There is a minimum threshold figure of £200,000 for each payment and the fee for the service is relatively high. We can be certain, therefore, that the majority of these transactions occur between financial institutions, though there will be some intermediate transactions between firms, and even some housing transactions. In a survey carried out for the Bank of England in 1996, APACS estimated that some 60 per cent of CHAPS transactions involved foreign exchange dealing. Given their composition, and given that CHAPS payments dominate the transactions aggregate, it is a reasonable inference to draw that financial transactions (especially perhaps foreign exchange transactions) increased very dramatically during the 1980s.

The Thatcher governments, like many others of the time, were ideologically committed to deregulation. This was especially true of their approach to the financial sector, and was something of a paradox given the simultaneous commitment to explicit monetary targets and strict monetary control (at least in the period 1980-85). Foreign exchange controls were removed in 1979 and this partly explains the explosion of foreign exchange business behind the rise in the multiple. In addition, major steps were taken to reduce the very tight restrictions on building societies' sources and uses of funds, to enable them to compete more closely with banks. The 1983 Finance Act enabled them to raise wholesale funds and to pay interest gross on wholesale borrowing. But the big breakthrough came in the 1986 Building Societies Act, which permitted, for the first time, a small amount of unsecured personal lending. This allowed building societies to issue cheque guarantee cards for the first time, turning their deposits into unambiguous means of payment overnight. Remarkably for demand deposits, they paid interest, and banks had then to follow suit. By 1990, virtually all positive balances paid interest. The effect can be seen in the decline of the non-interest bearing component of the money stock during the 1980s. At end-1982, the ratio of NIBM1 formed 11.8 per cent of M4, while at end-1992 it amounted to only 5.5 per cent.[2]

A subtle consequence of this battle for deposits, and one that is highly pertinent to our story, was that deposit rates crept closer to loan rates (though the gap was still very wide for most households). Though rarely remarked,[3] the narrowing of this 'spread' represents a reduction in the real cost of borrowing, since agents in deficit always have the choice of meeting that deficit by either new borrowing or drawing on existing savings. As the cost of using savings rises, the choice is tipped towards more borrowing.

More dramatic was the effect of competition on the non-pecuniary cost of borrowing. This could be seen in a number of ways. It could be measured to some degree by the steady rise in the loan/value and loan/income ratios used by all mortgage lenders (banks and building societies) in their assessment of creditworthiness. The average multiple of loan to household income rose from 1.64 in 1980 to 2.25 by 1992.[4] It could also be seen by the increase in high street stores acting as agents for banks in the promotion of instantly available consumer credit (aided by new communications technology which enabled real-time checking of credit-status), and in the avalanche of unsolicited offers of credit and credit cards through the post. A quantitative impression can be gained from the *Bank of England Quarterly Bulletin*'s periodic listing of the institutions to which the Bank has granted a banking licence. The newcomers in recent years are almost all 'non-financial' firms, an indication that the direction in which they have chosen to expand their business in recent years has caused them technically to become 'banks'. With all these developments in the ease with which credit could be obtained, the non-pecuniary or 'squirm' costs of credit fell sharply between 1975 (when bank personal loans were still something of a novelty) and the mid-1990s. Heavy promotional campaigns featuring 'flexible friends', and insisting that an idyllic holiday required only a bikini and a Barclaycard, succeeded in replacing the stigma of 'debt' with the status of 'credit'.

---

2. Bank of England, *Statistical Abstract*, 1992, part 2, tables 4 and 5.
3. Although see C. Sprenkle and M. H. Miller, 'The Precautionary Demand for Broad and Narrow Money', *Economica*, 47, 1980.
4. Council for Mortgage Lenders, *Housing Finance*, various issues, table D3.

Asset transactions and prices

How do these developments link to the explosion of non-output expenditures and the boom in asset transactions and prices? The answer comes in three stages. Firstly, competitive developments amongst deposit-taking institutions resulted during the 1980s in a dramatic rise in the flow of new borrowing and consequently in the stock of debt. In 1980, the personal sector's ratio of floating rate debt (roughly mortgages plus consumer credit) to annual income was 0.42. By 1992, this ratio had more than doubled to 0.98 and the Bank of England was growing alarmed at the number of mortgage defaults and at the effect that even a small rise in interest rates could have on households' disposable income.[5]

The second part of the answer involves the creation of money. At the start of the last millennium money, for those who used it, consisted of precious metals stamped with the authority of the monarch. The quantity in circulation depended upon such influences as the physical discovery of such metals and the sovereign's need for finance (usually for military adventures). The quantity was certainly independent of the level of economic activity. But the question of which assets function as money is a matter of social convention. After precious metals we became accustomed to tokens with little intrinsic value, and then, early last century, to banknotes. Through most of the twentieth century we became accustomed to bank deposits and then, during the 1980s, to building society deposits. (It is an interesting illustration of the power of social convention to define monetary assets that building society deposits were being widely used for a subset of payments even before 1986 - some years, therefore, before the UK Treasury and Bank of England got round to amending the official measures of money in 1989). As a result, we start the twenty-first century with a situation where money consists overwhelmingly of bank deposits (about 92 per cent of the M4 broad money stock). The bulk of a nation's spending power is therefore a liability of private sector, profit-making, institutions, whose concern for their shareholders comes a long way before their interest in national economic policy. Crucially, these liabilities are a by-product of that activity which generates the greater part of bank profits, the granting of credit. This arises inevitably (or 'through the balance sheet identity'

5. *Bank of England Quarterly Bulletins*: 'Personal Credit in Perspective' (Feb 1988), 'The Housing Market' (Feb 1989), 'Personal Credit Problems' (May 1989).

in the jargon), since borrowers can only bring a loan into existence by the act of paying someone with it. The consequence of the sharp rise in household debt has, inevitably, been a corresponding rise in liquidity. Relative to national income, the quantity of broad money roughly doubled between 1980 and 1990 (and has roughly doubled again since then).

The final part of our answer involves portfolio preferences. Money is created by the actions of borrowers. But how do we know that all this extra money is wanted? This is not the silly question that it seems, provided that we recognise that 'want' here means 'want to hold'. In this sense, the borrowers do not want the money. They have deficits to meet which they do precisely by passing the money directly to their creditors. The creditors will not hesitate to accept it as a means of payment for goods and services supplied, and doubtless will be pleased to find their receipts increasing over time. But our question remains: do they wish to *hold* the extra money as part of their total wealth portfolio? In orthodox theory, the answer depends upon a trade-off of risk and return. Additional quantities of an asset will only be brought into a portfolio if it shows a higher return (or lower risk) than the assets already there. This may happen because of the characteristics of the asset itself, or because something happens to cause the risk/return characteristics of existing assets to deteriorate. The latter must, perforce, be the result in the case of additional money, for the following reason.

It is a curious characteristic of money that it is very difficult to destroy. Since loans create deposits, repayment of loans (in excess of new loans being granted) will reduce the total quantity of money. But nothing else will. Attempts by individuals to shed money from their existing portfolios (by buying alternative assets, for example) will only succeed to the extent that others are willing to accept additional deposits (by selling alternative assets). In the aggregate, such actions must be self-defeating. Visualise, against this background, the doubling and doubling again of the broad money stock caused by the credit explosion of the last twenty years. The economy, of course, has expanded over that period and more output, employment and trade requires more monetary assets for payment purposes. But the measures take this into account: the money stock has quadrupled *relative to* GDP. Is there anything in money's risk/return characteristics to make it so much more attractive as a means of holding wealth? Undoubtedly, the payment of interest on an increasing proportion of deposits and the tendency of such deposit rates to be bid up relative to others both work in this direction. But these are marginal changes. Bank and building society deposits still have fundamentally the same characteristics as they did a generation ago. This is why we must look to changes in the characteristics of *other* assets as the mechanism which helps households adjust to the expanded money stock.

Confronted with a disproportionate share of their wealth in monetary form, households have pursued their individual self-interest by switching money into other assets. At various times since 1980 the favoured assets have been houses (three times) and company shares (twice). Since the supply of such assets is relatively fixed, their prices must rise. As we know, such behaviour is self-defeating in the aggregate, in the sense that it fails completely to reduce the supply of money. But it does have two crucially important side effects which work to encourage people to hold the expanded money stock willingly.

The first is that the rise in asset prices itself helps restore some degree of equilibrium. Portfolio structures are measured by value. If the *quantity* of money in a portfolio doubles, a doubling of the *price* of everything else brings us back to where we began. If the quantity of money quadruples, a fourfold rise in share prices maintains something of the original balance. The second is that a rise in the price of an asset, which is not accompanied by a simultaneous and equal rise in the value of the benefits which flow from it, *must* cause fall in the return available on that asset. This was the point which was made in the earlier arithmetic. A rise in share price (P), with dividends (D) static or rising more slowly, *must* cause dividend yields to fall. A rise in bond prices (their interest payments typically being fixed for their lifetime) *must* cause bond yields to fall. Thus, (failed) attempts to reduce money holdings by switching into these assets have the highly significant side effect of reducing their attractions relative to money. This is just a long way of saying that the extra money available begins to seem more attractive than it was when it first appeared.

In summary then, the transformation of credit supply conditions, and attitudes towards debt, have led in recent years to much higher levels of household debt. As a by-product, substantial money balances have also been created. Attempts to maintain a 'normal' portfolio structure have led to increased demands for alternative assets which are in generally fixed supply. Their inevitable price rise has helped maintain their portfolio share and made further attempts to swap them for money eventually unattractive.

Implications

Does any of this matter, beyond the confines of the economics seminar?

For the economy as a whole, the growth of asset trading can be seen as just one concrete illustration of the movement from secondary to tertiary activity, from production of goods to production of services. The growth of mutual funds, and the siting of LIFFE and the bulk of the European eurobond market in London, is just the contemporary equivalent of the growth of shipping insurance in the later nineteenth century. It is no different, analytically, from the growth of media, communications and some cultural industries that the UK has enjoyed in recent years. Provided that such services can be sold abroad in order to earn the means with which to pay for the import of the manufactured goods and raw materials that the economy does still need, there is no obvious problem in the aggregate. There is, of a course, a question about the ownership of skills and other endowments necessary to prosper from these developments, but we return to distributional questions later.

More subtly, it is not so satisfactory when lending institutions (as opposed to trading institutions) take the view that lending for asset trading is more profitable than lending for production of goods and services. When banks, with already a poor enough reputation for financing UK industry, switch, as a matter of policy, to lending for house purchase, and then try to benefit from housing transactions twice over by buying chains of estate agents, we might wonder about the enthusiasm with which productive activity is being served.

Thinking still of the economy as a whole, high asset prices mean low costs of capital. For a firm paying a given annual dividend it is much cheaper to raise new funds if investors are prepared to pay £4 for shares in a new issue than if the new shares can only be sold for £2. The danger, of course, is that these prices are not sustainable, and that firms are developing projects (using resources in the process) which will never be profitable at asset price (capital cost) levels which are, historically at least, more normal and may reappear in the future.

In the event of a crash, the nightmare possibility centres on the wealth effect of changing asset prices. It is a widely accepted hypothesis ('hypothesis' since empirical confirmation is scarce) that people are more willing to spend when they feel wealthy. If this is true, then a collapse in asset prices is likely to be followed quite quickly by a fall in consumer spending and then in firms' investment. Some firms will fail and unemployment will rise because of the lack of demand; and if asset prices fall far enough, firms with the wrong sort of assets on their balance sheets will fail because they are technically insolvent, even though they may be profitable. Such firms may typically be banks, which conjures up the spectre of contagious financial collapse. Fear of this doomsday scenario explains the speed with which central banks cut interest rates following the 1987 crashes and after the Asian crisis ten years later.

For a sight of the micro implications we need to go back to our opening paragraphs. The boom in asset prices in recent years has been very welcome to those fortunate enough to be holding the right assets, or to have sufficient surplus income (combined with an alertness to what is happening) to direct their savings appropriately and quickly. Considered carefully, the ownership of financial and housing assets during this long boom confers two fundamental benefits. The assets themselves are 'temporary abodes of purchasing power'. They can, after a short delay, be used to buy other assets or newly produced goods and services. An increase in *relative* wealth, such as the owners of these assets have enjoyed, amounts to an increase in their relative command of other resources, in much the same way as would follow from a shift in the distribution of income in their favour. The other benefit resides in any asset's ability to generate future income. As we saw earlier, its value is conventionally said to depend upon that ability. If assets are conventionally valued at the moment, then some people are going to enjoy an unearned income beyond the dreams even of their parents. And if they are not - if at some point a more 'normal' relationship between asset prices and incomes is re-established - the smart can still exploit the current level of prices to protect their future wealth by switching into assets of fixed nominal value.

Furthermore, if asset inflation exceeds nominal income growth for a number of years, the effects are cumulative. With asset returns of 34 per cent, an investor who draws the whole of the gain as income in one year will find that the portfolio reverts to its starting value. If the gain is 34 per cent next year, s/he can draw the same income, watching the portfolio revert again to its starting value. Income and capital *growth*, in other words, will be zero. But drawing only half of the gain as income, and reinvesting the rest in the same portfolio, will see *both* income and wealth grow at an annual rate of 17 per cent. The same arithmetic applies inexorably at levels of return. At a more reasonable long-run rate of 15 per cent, reinvesting half the gains will see income and wealth grow at 7½ per cent per annum, a rate which is substantially in excess of the likely growth in income from employment in the foreseeable future.

The relationship between borrower and lender, and the effect of this relationship upon the distribution of income and wealth, has always been complicated. On the face of it, concentrating solely on cashflows, borrowing results ultimately in a transfer of income from borrower to lender. Economists void the transaction of distributional significance by arguing that the borrower is having the benefit now of resources for which s/he would otherwise have to wait. Future repayments merely reverse the transaction and interest is what has to be paid to compensate those who postponed the exercise of *their* claim on resources in order to make it available to others. (Even so, there remains an interesting question as to the distributional effect of interest rate *changes*. A rise in interest rates, for example, increases the compensation paid to lenders even though there has been no change in the magnitude of resource claims passing between them).

B ut what we have seen in recent years makes the picture even more complicated. Let us suppose that the increase in borrowing is generally spread. More precisely, the ratio of outstanding debt to income increases in equal proportion across all income groups. (Official statistics do not allow us to check this, though it may be possible in future.) The consequence of this, we have seen, is a monetary expansion which has found its way more largely into asset purchases than into a demand for current production, with the result that asset prices have generally risen relative to those of goods and services. It seems unlikely that access to these assets is so democratically spread as the increase in debt. (Since official figures do not tell us much about liabilities by income group, neither do they tell us much about asset ownership.) Assume that the ownership of housing assets and equities is more restricted than 'ownership' of debt, and it is clear that borrowing has found a new way of redistributing income.

Conclusions

The last twenty or so years have seen a number developments in the UK economy, many of them ascribed to some sort of 'golden age' of deregulation, initiated by early Thatcher governments and endorsed it seems by New Labour. From the financial point of view, the removal of foreign exchange controls was undoubtedly a major step towards exposing the UK economy to the benefits as well as the costs of large-scale international capital flows. But other regulatory changes were important as well, especially those which lowered the demarcations between deposit-taking institutions and began a period of competition for deposits and lending which continues to this day. One effect of this competition has been to lower the cost of credit, to make it more readily available and to change cultural attitudes towards indebtedness. A consequence has been a sharp rise in household indebtedness and a corresponding increase in the quantity of money (both of these increases are in relation to other variables like incomes and production). If such extra liquidity is not being used to finance production, it is being held as an asset and as such must take its place in portfolios alongside other financial assets. An increase in money for this purpose must in turn lead to an increase in demand for other financial assets if normal portfolio balance is to be maintained. Hence we have seen a substantial rise in asset prices, also relative to production and incomes. The implications are many, interesting and complex. In the last few years, it has not been difficult for people with modest wealth to earn a net return which matched income from employment (depending, of course, upon their job and on their ability to spot what was happening). Such asset price increases may be unsustainably dramatic. But a long-run effect upon the distribution of income and wealth is perfectly plausible. Provided governments succeed in keeping measured inflation in low single figures, and provided the measure is based upon the costs of production and output, asset price inflation of quite modest historical proportions will ensure that income from wealth rises more rapidly than income from employment.

Between you and me

Living with difference

Emma Satyamurti

Emma Satyamurti reflects on the effects disability can have on one's sense of identity.

Arriving in the hotel lobby I felt deeply ambivalent. My attendance at the annual convention of the Restricted Growth Association represented a departure from years of resistance to the idea of deliberately seeking out the company of other disabled people. I have a rare genetic condition called multiple pterygium syndrome, among whose most visible effects are stiff joints, curvature of the spine and, above all, small stature - I am four feet tall. But it is not the physical symptoms of my syndrome which cause me the greatest difficulty. One of the most problematic features of my disability has been the psychological task of reconciling the normal and abnormal aspects of my life.

From as far back as I can remember, suggestions that I might like to try out this or that group for disabled people - swimming, socials, and the RGA itself - have filled me with such disproportionate feelings of panic and rebellion that finally I could not deny, even to myself, the irrationality of my position. I began to wonder why it was that even the idea of fraternising with other physically abnormal people felt like such an attack on my sense of self, so that actually going to a disabled club would have seemed a surrender of the most desperate kind.

A particular event in mid-childhood radically changed my attitude towards being disabled; since then I have felt my disability and my sense of self to be contradictory and mutually exclusive. When I was seven, my teacher encouraged me to take part in a 'walking race' at the school sports day. I still remember the shy feeling of astonishment and pride with which I crossed the finishing line first. I was delighted by the implication that, in one physical arena at least, I could participate on an equal footing with my peers. Some days later, my friend confessed that the class had been told to let me win.

I don't doubt that Miss G acted with good intentions, but the effect on me was profound. Before that point, the significance to me of my disability had simply been that I was functionally different from my classmates. Although they were more physically robust than I was and could leap about at playtime with abandon, I never doubted that I was one of the clan - that I belonged. The discovery that my sporting success had been staged, and the humiliation of having publicly owned a victory that everyone but me knew was unreal, spiralled me into a new insecurity. It was not the realisation that I was not a fast walker that was so deeply undermining, but the experience of finding that my carefree assumption that I was an equal participant in the society of my schoolmates - my strong belief in my own normality - might be rooted in a lie.

The shock of having been seen by so many to be something I had not known I was, engendered an equation in my mind between disability and loss of self which I am only now beginning to dismantle. Either I was not seen as 'disabled' by others, or the feeling for me which others professed was necessarily a conspiracy to make a disabled girl feel better. I did not think it possible to be thought of both as disabled and as a person like any other, and so expended a great deal of effort on keeping at bay my consciousness of my physical difference, a kind of psychological stiffening of the throat to avoid tasting something disgusting. Like the cat who fancies itself invisible when hiding only its head under a chair, I clung to the belief that if I could make the disability unreal to me, I could, by that effort of will, reduce its vividness for others.

Paradoxically, this strategy of avoiding the issue both worked and failed. It encouraged people to focus on the person rather than the disability, but it also created an area of silence which sharpened their curiosity, and circumscribed the intimacy that was possible between us. I have often discovered - years into a friendship - that there were many questions waiting to be asked. But whatever the outcome, the denial of my disability seemed to me essential to the survival of an autonomous identity. I felt it as an ever-present danger that if I yielded at all to the pressure of what I was denying, I would find my self buried alive in a box labelled 'invalid'. Consequently, any feelings of loss or frustration connected with being disabled must be suppressed.

But here I was, standing on the edge of a room full of people whose defining feature was their Lilliputian stature and experience of physical difference. I felt both exhilaration at the prospect of finding that I was not unique, and also fear of making exactly that discovery: that I belonged to a group sharing the very identity I had felt might extinguish me - 'the disabled'. Although I felt nervous about acknowledging my disability, and by seeing some aspects of it reflected in others (and indeed once during the weekend had to call a friend as a reassurance that my 'normal' life still existed), excitement was the dominant feeling with which I entered the room. It derived from the anticipated relief of meeting people among whom I might feel less visually extraordinary than in any other social context, and of perhaps learning something about their experience of being different.

My childhood shock at finding myself looked at in a way over which I had no control, suddenly alienated when I had felt no separation between me and my seven-year-old peers, has manifested itself since adolescence in the belief that my disability must make me physically grotesque. Despair in front of the mirror is an almost universally familiar emotion, among the more and less beautiful alike. But the concrete abnormalities of my syndrome made it particularly hard to rescue some hope of acceptability or even attractiveness.

It is tempting to attribute blame for this to the beauty propaganda which shimmers from countless billboards, and certainly this does little to calm the fear that one is beyond the aesthetic pale. But, for me, the tyranny of conventional models of beauty merely contributed to a self-protective, though ultimately unhelpful, emotional strategy that I developed for living with difference. The absence of anyone in whose image I find myself reflected makes particularly painful the impossibility of controlling the perceptions of others - and therefore of keeping my sense of self safe. Like the singular Bunyip in the children's story, who wanders the earth asking 'What am I?', I simply do not know what others see, how my oddness is received. Am I a freak of nature and accordingly deeply disconcerting? Or do I simply occupy the more extreme end of the continuous spectrum of human variation? Although I am lucky in the encouragement and affirmation of many friends whose sincerity I trust, the impossibility of any final reassurance that I am not, in my disability, potentially disturbing has been one of the most pervasive realities of my daily life.

Intellectually I know that, because weirdness, like beauty, lies partly in the eye of the beholder, I should not mind the astonishment my appearance often provokes. But in that moment of surprise I feel changed, an experience perhaps common to anyone who finds themselves outside the normality of the world around them. The expressions of incredulity - covert in adults, frank in children - which frequently follow me down the street make the emotional leap from feeling that I am simply different, to the conviction that I am transgressively other, difficult to resist.

For the discomfort of others I have an antidote - conversation. Like many people with disabilities, I have become adept at building bridges out of words, which is, I suppose, a way of re-establishing the common ground. The remedy of speech, however, is not so effective against my own dis-ease at what I imagine I become in the gaze of others. Logically, if I feel transformed by the initial amazement some people's faces betray, I ought to feel restored to myself in sensing the fading of my strangeness to them as talk passes between us. But, in fact, I don't. The memory of the first stare, eloquently conveying the question 'What is that?', is what stays.

The alternative antidote I have developed to diminish my own discomfort has, I now realise, the unfortunate side effect of also diminishing both me and the people I encounter. Rather than tolerate the constant shock of seeing myself distorted in the expressions of strangers, I have, barely consciously, come to believe, myself, that I am a distortion. In an attempt to control the disjunction between my sense of self - a self free from a disabled body - and the emphatically embodied figure I represent to others, I impute disgust to others as a matter of routine. To imagine the worst is, at least partially, to limit the power of those under whose scrutiny one falls; one can be confirmed in one's pessimism, but cannot be taken by surprise. But this negative attitude is also, of course, cynical. To assume revulsion where there may be only confusion or surprise, does little justice to the decency and humanity most people possess (and indeed I know from my own experience of seeing unusual people that the fact of being struck by a person's difference need imply nothing more than interest). This interaction between other people's responses and what I make of them represents the most powerfully disabling consequence of my disability.

But perhaps it doesn't have to be like that. After all, second-guessing is a singularly pointless exercise. Either a person is responding to one negatively, in which case anticipating that response has not prevented it; or there has been no such reaction, and yet one has given oneself grief nevertheless.

A few weeks ago, a builder came to repair my roof. Usually if I am arranging a meeting with someone I have not met, I try to find a natural way of alerting them to the fact that there is something 'wrong' with me, feeling that it is somehow unfair that they should be confronted by my disability unprepared. On this occasion no opportunity had presented itself, and before he arrived I felt I had somehow tricked him by not giving him any hint of the person who would answer the door. In the event he was not visibly fazed, but the old worry surfaced. Was he just good at hiding consternation?

In case he was, I was extra keen to put him at ease with animated conversation and tea. One of the things I first noticed about him was the number of lurid tattoos covering his arms. Later it emerged that he had had them done as a teenager and now, in middle age, bitterly regretted them, feeling they were an eyesore and made people react to him in ways that he felt did not reflect the person he now was. It was not possible to have them removed. So, like me, he sat at the table uncomfortable in his skin, despite the fact that he was a strong and well-built man.

Paradoxically, while Pete and I hit it off like a roof on fire in our mutual insecurity, at the RGA conference I felt peripheral. Where I had naively expected the company of other small people to help me achieve a greater psychological integration, I felt no less awkward than usual, despite the warmth and openness with which I was welcomed. But perhaps that is as it should be. Although, after years of searching, the Bunyip in the story finds happiness in the discovery of another Bunyip, in life there are, of course, no simple answers. An identity is, perhaps, not something to be arrived at once and for all, but, rather, a lifelong process of experience and response. The pain so many of us feel when confronted by the gap - real or imagined - between our self perception and the reflection of ourselves we get back from the world, is, I think, greatly intensified by seeing life as a series of stills. Each moment of unwelcome attention, humiliation, belittlement, seems captured forever, acquiring a separate reality that can be cringed over at length. It is a poignant fact that although our eyes are positioned for looking out into the world, many of us ruin this advantage by habitually turning our mind's eye on ourselves in an attempt to see what others do.

But feeling at ease about one's place in the world (and, in that sense, having a healthy identity) may depend on taking a view of life as more like flowing water. Left to itself, life moves forwards in a continuous succession of experiences. But in my, certainly not unique, experience, anxiety creates, as it were, turbulence, interfering with the smooth passage of the stream. Although, unlike in the story, there may be nothing as clear cut as a happy ending, directing one's eyes, and energy, outwards may make floating easier.

Five poems

They say you never forget

but by the time they got round to it
caution had doused what ardour
they'd started with. *Nice girls*
don't. Nice girls keep something
in reserve. Like a nest egg.
And his failure to ask a barber.

So they were just good friends, abroad
with a crowd when their car stalled
throwing them back on each other -
no transport and just enough money
for a single room, shuttered
against the heat and mosquitoes.

It must have happened. She remembers
weeks later, on a bus in London,
wondering, if - would she marry him?
And the car up on hoists. And the bed,
how those black grains bit and bled
when you caught and crushed them.

Of course she remembers. That room.
Waiting for a big end to be flown over.
Just bread and red wine and sweating
making up crosswords for each other.
Forty years, as if it were yesterday.
It's only the sex she's forgotten.

Frances Wilson

one up by clayton

Upstate they handled drought their own ways
this year. They broke off corn stalks, picked
clods and winnowed them through their fingers
on all three major networks, and *Nightline*.

One up by Clayton used a .22 to make
a hole over his left eye. The half-
hour it took for him to die, he slammed
against the etagère, knocked the clock

with the passage of scripture off the wall.
He fell to the rug, got up. He held on
to the latch and bent over at the back door
for at least a minute, like he was thinking,

like he was studying the dull boards
in the floor, how they were starting
to separate. He went outside and wiped
a cobweb off the post that was coming loose

on the porch. He sat on the last step.
He walked to the gate, dropped his wallet
through the grating on the cow-catcher.
He crossed the road and leaned on the Bixby

mailbox, hard, then died in the run-off.
There wasn't any mystery to it. On the local
stations, his friends knew exactly what happened
by what he broke, or smeared. Where he'd started to bruise.

Paul Allen

Writing on Skin

You urge me to use my blunt nail on your skin.
Just any word. I can't think, then start 'V' -
a downstroke. Lift. Another. The drag of skin
under my index finger. 'E – I – N'.

There's nothing there to see. Invisible ink.
Like when, a kid, I was into lemon juice
for spy stuff, words that dried unseeable
and needed a flame to turn them sepia.

… *eleven, twelve* … you're counting, and now 'VEIN'
is burning through like on a polaroid.
Thin rosy weals on the parchment of your wrist.
The word I've chosen, written in my hand.

Catherine Byron

Mouthpiece

Now the boys are men, this spring
as I'm clearing the holly clump,
as I saw down the last leggy trunk
crowding the walnut's branches,
among what's left, the grey-green
wands with their snipped-off white ends,
the recorder mouthpiece turns up:
besmirched with dirt but apparently
undamaged by the years outdoors,
a plastic toy I'd forgotten,
like the almost flat platform once wedged
in the walnut tree overhead
where the boys would keep watch for Kay
and passers-by over the hedge
and whistle shrill warnings. It won't
let the air pass freely, resists me,
must be choked with leaf mould or something.
But I won't take no for an answer,
I take a deep breath and blow
harder, make a weak treble peep.

Michael Laskey

Miscarriage at Eleusis*

They exhume what remains of me at Eleusis
a voracious, undead, scrabbling Thing, buried too quickly under
marble.
Mystery. Parting from Her into secrets and a first darkness of
little girl love, sticky
sheets, sacred greed for Him.
Then, horror. The echo of her voice.
No. Not here. Forbidden here. A ghastly mushrooming of pale
breasts, milky breath,
musky mother smell
into my body's ancient taboo.
Lights flare on. A short struggle I could never win and I curl in
defeat.
He lies deflated. Shrunk to a photograph in a fan magazine.
She annexes it, hides it in a secret place. Smacks my hand, then
kisses it and
rests it against her face.
I drop like spore from ripe fungus. Settle back into her womb,
swell there, a blighted embryo. Big head, big blind eyes.
When she dies, I will be surgically removed, knocked on the
head and buried,
ravenous, at Eleusis.
Sssh! It's a female mystery.

Susie Campbell

* The Eleusinian Mysteries celebrated the restoration of Persephone to her
mother Demeter after her abduction. Persephone's child by the god of the
Underworld represents fertility and a resolution of conflict between mother
goddess and male god.

New Labour and constitutional reform

Why not introduce compulsory voting in all elections?

G. C. Harcourt

G.C. Harcourt *argues that compulsory voting would be a good way for New Labour to promote the responsibilities of citizenship.*

New Labour, though keen to reform the United Kingdom constitution (or lack of it), has never considered one obvious, simple constitutional change which is democratically desirable and helpful to New Labour's cause - the introduction of compulsory voting in all elections. When I first came to the United Kingdom in 1955 as a research student in economics at King's College, Cambridge, I was amazed to learn that voting was voluntary, not compulsory as it was in my native Australia. (That the polling day was on Thursday, a working week day, at least for part of it, not on Saturday, was also a surprise.)

Why do I think compulsory voting is a good thing in a democratic society? Let me first make explicit that voters under such a system would be fined if they did not turn up to vote (if they also failed to apply for an absentee vote);

but they would not be penalised if they spoilt their ballots because they did not wish to vote for anyone or any party. It would still after all be a secret ballot and only the voters would know what they had done in the polling booths. In spite of this, informal votes, as these are called, do not under such systems amount to anywhere near the proportion of people who do not bother to vote in voluntary voting systems. (Moreover, part of the informal vote results from people having been unable to follow the (usually simple) instructions on how to vote, i.e. how to fill in the ballot paper.) Compulsory voting is a good thing because by finding out the views of virtually the entire eligible voting populations, we get, probably as near as is possible in an imperfect world, a true sense of people's preferences.

In Australia, of course, compulsory voting for the House of Representatives in the Federal Parliament is coupled with preference voting for individual candidates and parties. So the ultimate outcome of an election often depends on second preferences. For example, when the Australian Labor Party (ALP, note the historically determined spelling of Labor) split in the 1950s, the right-wing, anti-Communist, Roman Catholic faction formed a separate party, the Democratic Labour Party (DLP) and gave their second preferences to the Liberal (read Conservative) Country Party coalition. This resulted in the ALP being out of government for 23 years.

A further feature of Australian elections is that the party faithful hand out 'How to vote' cards to voters as they arrive (at a legally determined distance from the polling booths). The hope is that the voters will follow the suggestions of their party and so stop preference drift occurring. By and large this is successful, though there is always a minority of donkey voters who just vote 1, 2, 3 ... down the card. This favours persons whose last names begin with 'A'; and they have a better chance of being selected by their party, especially during those years when a candidate's party affiliation was not put on the ballot paper. In 1961 the Menzies government nearly went out following a credit squeeze that got out of control and raised unemployment to above 2% (!!!!). A North Queensland conservative was elected as a result of donkey vote 'preferences' for the communist candidate Aarons, and this allowed the re-election of the Menzies government with a majority of one! Despite these examples, I think the Australian procedure is a good one; but I will not argue for its introduction in the United Kingdom as I want to concentrate on the prior need to have compulsory voting, and on the merits of this system. But I

ought perhaps to point out that if the UK had compulsory voting *and* the Australian preference voting system, and if New Labour gave its second preferences to the Liberal Democrats, and if the Lib-Dems returned the compliment, and if their voters followed the 'How to vote' cards, I do not see how the Conservatives could ever form a government again! In Australia, who the Democrats give their preferences to (they are similar to the Lib-Dems - too decent to be Tory, too snobby to be Labour) - can be vital for the outcome.

An implicit assumption in the case for voluntary voting is that, regardless of income or social class, or other defining characteristics of groups of voters, getting to vote is the same, as easy and as difficult, for everyone. But this is

'compulsory voting would produce, at one stroke, a level playing field for all'

clearly nonsense. The scales are inevitably weighted against the least privileged members of the community. As they are the ones most likely to vote for the more progressive parties, there is an in-built bias against the latter and in favour of the more conservative parties. Voting on weekdays has a similar effect, though now that the weekend blurs imperceptibly into the week this may not be as important. At one stroke, compulsory voting would produce that most sought after of modern institutions, a level playing field for all. Of course, initially, it would be unwise to stress the advantage that compulsory voting offers to New Labour; but it is reasonable to point out that the resulting level playing field is a valid argument if we want elections that more truly reflect the overall preferences of voters.

There have been a number of disquieting trends in democratic countries in recent decades, which compulsory voting would do something to offset. The most marginalised and least privileged groups have ceased to vote, in disproportionate numbers, because philosophical trends and the distribution of power, income and prosperity have combined to mean, increasingly, that governments can ignore their needs. We have a cumulative, self-fulfilling process, which is inequitable, socially destabilising and dangerous. If these groups had to vote, even within the structures of modern democratic capitalist societies, more emphasis would need to be put on their situation, as all parties would then be competing for their votes. An individual vote is, of course, neither here nor there and does not count. But, collectively, votes can make a difference. We have a classic case of the fallacy of composition - what I do

in isolation has a different outcome from that which will result when all 'I's do it at the same time.

In an ideal world no doubt, voluntary voting would be preferable - witness the inspiring sight of South Africans lining up to vote in the first election of the post-apartheid regime, an action of vital significance and importance for those who previously had been disenfranchised. It was a sight which ought to have shamed the United Kingdom's often apathetic and cynical voters, especially those who do not bother to vote or even inform themselves about what the issues are and how each party proposes to tackle them. An unwillingness to vote is an awful judgement on the present state of society, reflecting the decline in communal solidarity and the lack of appreciation of past struggles to gain this basic right.

I suspect it is partly a by-product of the rise of the self-interested individual associated with the Thatcher years (the decline in social capital is the current buzz words phrase) - there is a widespread assumption that the only person to look after is yourself and perhaps your immediate family, and that misfortune is by and large the fault of those who suffer it. After all, capitalism is institutionalised greed and selfishness, and modern vulgar followers of Adam Smith (of the *Wealth of Nations*) forget - they probably never knew - that his precondition for the viability and beneficial effects of a competitive economy in which self-interest guided decisions and actions was the prior creation of institutions which fostered altruism in various dimensions of social life, often through government measures. This was the central theme of his *Theory of Moral Sentiments*. (Smith was not, of course, a democrat - in his book, Demos is *at best*, placed third, with Philosopher Kings (no queens) in second place, and rank and wealth first. Perhaps he would have supported New Labour?)

New Labour is always stressing individual responsibility in return for individual rights. This surely implies that a requirement to vote would be the first responsibility of a citizen of a society with a democratic constitution, and the benefits which that bestows. As Michael Rustin (26.6.2000) says of this: 'The main thing is that they should have to make the effort to carry out their civic responsibility'.

The argument for compulsory voting is strong for general elections; it is perhaps even stronger for European and local elections where turn-outs are abysmal, as they have tended to be also for some of the new devolved assemblies.

Australians and Australian society are very democratic, for all our faults, and one reason for this is, I believe, that we are required to exercise our democratic rights by compulsory voting in both Federal and State elections. (These are held more frequently than corresponding elections in the United Kingdom, probably too frequently to allow for the implementation of sound and thoughtful economic and social policies.) The United Kingdom, again for all its faults, has pioneered the creation of some of the institutions which characterise democratic societies, not least the creation of an uncorrupt civil service - another institution which is not properly valued in modern Britain. Compulsory voting seems an obvious, simple and desirable change which would help to begin the task of offsetting current cynical and apathetic trends - which could ultimately destroy what the pioneers of democracy began to create.

I am most grateful to Michael Rustin for asking me to write this essay and for setting out arguments on which I have freely drawn.

Posoltega

Paulette Goudge

Paulette Goudge discusses the shortcomings of western responses to third world emergencies.

I wanted to go to Posoltega. I was in Nicaragua for a five week stay over Christmas 1999 to visit old friends and to see how things were working out, and I was keen to spend the millennium in a place where complete absence of the Dome would be assured. Posoltega is a small community in north western Nicaragua, which became one of those events which catapults an otherwise small and insignificant 'Third World' country into the headlines of the British press, when, on 30 October 1998 a vast mudslide, one of the deadly consequences of Hurricane Mitch, devastated the region. People had precisely seven seconds from the moment they heard the first rumble foretelling that the volcano was about to blow to the moment the mud-flow hit them. Seven seconds in which to try to save themselves and their children.

Like many others in Britain who know Nicaragua personally and have contacts there, I felt deeply affected, and became almost obsessed with the updates of the rising figures of the dead and dispossessed, and the pictures of destruction which for a while were broadcast on a daily basis and transmitted via e-mail. I became quite frantic for a day or two, concerned for the fate of friends and acquaintances, and rushed about doing my bit to raise as much awareness and cash as possible.

I am interested in how development aid works. And having seen the graphic photographs of the impact of the mudslide devouring everything in its path, I wanted to see how the aid agencies had responded and how effectively they were repairing the damage. That, at least, was the conscious motive for my journey to Posoltega.

So I wanted to go and I wanted to interview people affected by the hurricane. I was lucky inasmuch as an old friend from Britain is working for a British NGO and is actually living in Posoltega. I persuaded her to introduce me to people

Petronella and her adopted son

whom she thought would have something interesting to say. The first person she took me to visit was Petronella.

Petronella has been interviewed several times before, and because of this my friend was a little reluctant to 'use her like that again'. I like to think retelling her story to me was helpful to her. I also prefer to repress the memory that returns to me now as I write that I terminated the interview in something of a hurry as a taxi was waiting to return me to town. She won't read this or, unless I make a special effort, see the photo I took of her and her adopted son. I shall tell her story in the hope that it validates in some way my exploitation of her experiences and feelings.

Her father, husband and three daughters were swept away during the mudslide in Posoltega. For several days she did not know their fate, searching for them, hoping against hope that they would turn up alive somewhere. A neighbour told her that bodies were being held in a convent and that three of them fitted the description of her children. She travelled there, but was not allowed to see if her daughters were among the dead.

Petronella now takes care of two children who were orphaned during the hurricane. They live in the tents of Santa Maria, where 350 families are still awaiting the first sign of a new house. Many people are in black plastic tents - in the heat of the day it is like entering an oven. No school has been built - but Petronella, together with some of the other parents, does her best to teach the children on a voluntary basis.

As well as teaching, Petronella also does heavy manual work clearing the land for eighty hours a month. This is in exchange for her family's basic rations - 8lb of beans, maize and 4 litres of oil per month. They used to get rice as well; she is not sure why that stopped. She earns no money and therefore cannot buy soap or clothes or vegetables, and is dependent on handouts for such 'extras'. This is the 'Work for Basic Necessities Scheme' which provides the only source of employment for most of the dispossessed families.

Over sixty non-governmental organisations (both Nicaraguan and international) have been involved in the region since October 1998. Nevertheless, there is no free or regularly available healthcare. Petronella showed me an injury to Daniel's head (the nine-year-old she has adopted), sustained when he crashed into a tree as he was swept away by the force of the mudslide. She does not have the 100 cordobas (about £8) to pay for the X-ray which her doctor considers essential.

Whilst I was in Santa Maria, word went round that a doctor from one of the NGOs was visiting. He would be there for the afternoon and would see fifty people on a first come, first served, basis. No-one knew where the message had come from, or whether the doctor would return. Petronella thought that if she hurried she might be lucky and get her injured foot seen.

1400 families were made homeless by the mudslide. Sixteen months later, 225 have been re-housed. Another 122 houses were started in January 2000. One aid worker told me that, as time goes by, it gets harder for the NGOs to decide who are the 'real survivors' of the hurricane - and therefore 'deserving' of re-housing - and who are the 'hangers on', who only want a new house because of the standard reasons of poverty.

The hurricane hit an area of Nicaragua which was already ecologically and economically very fragile. Until the 1980s the agricultural basis of the region was cotton, but this was completely devastated by the slump in world prices, leaving behind a legacy of soil so full of pesticides that nothing else can be planted. The local industry of embroidered cotton shirts has, in the process, also been destroyed. Many people, whether directly affected by the hurricane or not, are experiencing life way below the poverty line. The NGOs assess some as more deserving than others.

Raul Martinez is Director of the Health Centre in Posoltega. In the first days after the hurricane no help arrived from either the Nicaraguan government or the NGOs. He, together with some local volunteers and students from the nearby town of Leon, went from house to house giving everyone they could find a bottle of chlorine and advice on how to avoid cholera and leptospirosis. That was how an epidemic was avoided. And this was in the context of disease generally being on the increase in Nicaragua. (For example, in 1999 there were 6000 more cases of malaria than in 1998.)

At the same time, this 32 year old, with the assistance of the local Chief of Police, had the responsibility of supervising the burning of 2500 human bodies, as well as disposing of decomposing cattle, horses, pigs, chickens. Even now, when they get together socially, their main topic of conversation is the pain and anguish of this task. It took two months to complete.

One eighth of Posoltega's population was killed.

After a few days, the NGOs began to arrive. Of the 60 operating in the area, 20 of them were concerned with health. Some of them informed Raul of their presence and their plans. Others did not. Some of them attended meetings designed to co-ordinate objectives and resources. Others did not. One or two asked Raul what help he needed to carry out his job more effectively in the circumstances, but most did not. He showed me the cupboard where the out-of-date (some by years) drugs donated by the First World are stored. He remembers a Minister from England visiting in a helicopter and flying over the town. The helicopter did not land. In Santa Maria he says there are so many organisations that he has no idea who is who and who is doing what.

The different organisations are most visible in the small town centre of Posoltega, where the aid workers sport distinctive NGO logos on the sides of their four-wheeled vehicles and T-shirts. One aid worker commented to me that the giving of presents to children at Christmas seemed to owe most to good photo opportunities.

Having lunch in Alejandra's eating place in Posoltega, I notice that, as well as cooking and serving food, she is handing out bars of medicated soap to the customers. Nobody requests it and it is received without comment. Alejandra tells me it's a donation which just arrived, she does not know where from. She doesn't quite know what she is supposed to do with it, so she gives it to whoever happens to be passing through. There may well be trouble later when the soap is all gone, but word has got around and people turn up looking for their free gift. I hear other stories of donations just arriving out of nowhere and people fighting over plastic chairs, sewing machines, cooking pots and other necessities. Raul comments that the increasing culture of dependency on aid is undermining the local community.

The last words should go to Petronella and Raul. Petronella smiles as she says she is hopeful that the government and some of the NGOs are co-operating more now, and that perhaps the year 2000 will see them work together sufficiently to start building a proper school for the community of Santa Maria. Raul's hope for the new Millennium is that the outsiders who arrive, well meaning and well resourced, will 'ask us rather than tell us what we need'. Moved by their stories I say my farewells; above all I am deeply impressed by their continual optimism that things can and will improve in their lives and those of their neighbours.

Sanitising South Africa

Simon Lewis

Post-apartheid South Africa remains a paradise for the wealthy, most of whom display a convenient amnesia in relation to the country's history.

The end of apartheid appeared to be one of those pivotal moments of virtually epochal change. The advent of 'freedom' in South Africa has been rather more equivocal, however, than the iconic images of a smiling, newly-suited, clenched-fisted Nelson Mandela suggest - or those snaking multiracial, multilingual, multiparty election lines. As a particularly blunt example, let me cite a conversation reported to me by a publisher friend in London a matter of months after the release of Nelson Mandela. This friend had been attending a dinner party at which a member of the English landed gentry had welcomed the prospect of freedom in South Africa with surprising warmth - on the grounds that it would open up a new market for *Penthouse* magazine. Where the crowds greeting Mandela on his release and waiting in line at the polling stations were celebrating the near-miraculous possibility of political freedom, and the chance to participate in building a new nation, the business community both locally and internationally breathed a sigh of relief that, by avoiding revolution or civil war, they would be able to achieve what Patrick Bond has called an 'élite transition',[1] under which the more things changed, the more they would stay the same (see figure 1). Above all, they would be able to hold on to their privileges, among which,

---

1. Patrick Bond, *The Elite Transition: From Apartheid to Neoliberalism in South Africa*, Pluto, London 1999.

Figure 1: cultural and physical indicators of change/lack of change in contemporary South Africa (most, but not all of the examples are elucidated in the article)

PLUS ÇA CHANGE	PLUS C'EST LA MEME CHOSE
(almost all local)	(eyes on the international)
1. Cultural	
testimony of previously silenced voices at TRC	renewed confidence in significance of sport, expenditure of money on organised leisure
oral history projects - eg van Onselen's life of sharecropper Kas Maine	recycling of old images (wild animals, exotic landscape, hunting/ photography)
revisionary social histories - eg Worden et al, (eds) *Cape Town*	'world in one country' - emphasis on natural variety (including anthropological variety), rather than SA as working space
new museums - eg Robben Island	
revised museum displays, new styles of museum display	
mainstreaming of interest in previously marginalised figures – 'Hottentots', (Krotoa Sara Baartman), 'Bushmen', Cape Malays, slaves	morphing of embarrassingly unacceptable legislated racial exclusivity into acceptable class exclusivity
upsurge of new (sub-)nationalisms (Coloured, Griqua)	re-release of 'safe' liberal material (*Cry, the Beloved Country, Ipi Tombi*)
2. Physical	
provision of low-cost housing, medical facilities, etc	gated communities

apparently, must be counted the gentlemanly privilege of purveying and consuming pornography.

That the idea of 'freedom' implied in the term 'free trade', on the one hand, and 'political freedom', on the other, might be different is perhaps obvious, but the difference is strikingly acute in contemporary South Africa, where the desire to sell the country abroad as safely sanitised rainbow nation can appear like selling out to those cultural workers - policy-makers, historians, teachers, writers, artists - who see the local processes of remaking and re-presenting South Africa as ongoing projects of considerable urgency, complexity, and precariousness, projects in which the often uncomfortable de-sanitising of apartheid era stories and images plays a key role. Over the decade since Mandela's release, with abstract freedoms now apparently enshrined in an exemplary constitution and its accompanying civil institutions, the gap between entrepreneurial empire-builders and community-minded nation-builders has, if anything, been widening. While historians and artists, and state-supported programmes like the Truth and Reconciliation Commission, have been labouring to create a 'new' South Africa that can come to terms with its violent past and the suppressions and misrepresentations of that past, South African business has tended to want to take 1994 as a marker of an end of history or an end of politics. With apartheid now formally 'dealt with', they would like to be free to say, aping Calvin Coolidge, 'the business of South Africa is business'.

S uch exclusive concern with bottom-lines - of historic periods or balance sheets - is clearly driven by self-interest. As early as 1996, in a poem called 'Even the Dead', the poet-activist Jeremy Cronin was attacking the various kinds of amnesia that have allowed South Africa's business leaders to maintain their wealth and privilege, while urging (or perhaps *by* urging) 'all South Africans to bury the past unconditionally'. Cronin's commitment to an activist role for poetry becomes plain when we recognise that the material of the poem corresponds with the material included in the South African Communist Party's submission to the Truth and Reconciliation Commission.[2] Through its very different medium

---

2. See the article 'Harvesting Apartheid' in *African Communist* 148, which comprises the November 1997 SACP report to the TRC hearings on 'Business and Apartheid'. The references to Joggie Heuser and the TRC, identical to those used in 'Even the Dead', suggest that Cronin, in his capacity as deputy general secretary of the party, was at least co-author of the report.

the poem is a passionate general plea to art to help the people stay awake and not suffer from the 'globalised amnesia' of CNN, the 'lobotomised amnesia' of the Gulf War, and the 'milk of amnesia' of American soap-operas; but its particular concern is with the local South African amnesias that allow the burial of past economic exploitation even as the actual bodies of apartheid violence are being exhumed.

The poem concludes with sombre endorsement of a quotation from Walter Benjamin: 'Only that historian will have the gift of fanning some sparks of hope in the past who is firmly convinced that even the dead will not be safe from the enemy if he wins. And this enemy has not ceased to be victorious'. While voices like Cronin's now have more officially sanctioned outlets in the South African media and culture from which they had previously been barred, such voices have by no means displaced the old. Indeed, there are other perhaps more insidious signs of amnesiac accommodation to the new-old order, which indicate the continuity of a way of seeing the land in terms of landscape and property, of gentlemen and their exclusive penthouses, mansions and estates.

Since the system of apartheid was a system of spatial control, it is not surprising that much of the revisionist work of politicians, historians and artists concerns space - whether in the renaming of place-names, provision of new housing, production of revisionist local histories, or acutely localised films, plays, novels or museum displays dealing with previously taboo subjects (such as slavery in John Badenhorst's film *Slavery of Love* or incest in a poor white Afrikaner family in Marlene van Niekerk's *Triomf*).[3] What all these efforts share is Cronin's determination to resist amnesia, and to recognise, in photographer David Goldblatt's words, that 'the structure of things then'[4] has marked and is still marking the landscape of South Africa. The 'new' South Africa has to re-imagine itself within a space that has been arranged as if the entire nation were a giant industrial/agricultural plantation with designated areas for masters and servants. Such reimagining is not easy when the material traces of symbolic power remain

3. For an excellent compilation of work on this topic see Sarah Nuttall and Carli Coetzee (eds), *Negotiating the Past: The Making of Memory in South Africa*, Oxford University Press, Cape Town 1998.
4. See David Goldblatt, *South Africa: The Structure of Things Then*, Monacelli, New York 1998.

intact both physically and discursively.

For instance, at the same time that academics and artists are producing their challenging revisionist work, many tour operators and real estate agents are blithely selling South Africa abroad as if it were fully rehabilitated already, all too willing to forget the past which blighted tourism and international trade in the last years of apartheid. Apparently unconcerned with presenting images of a new South Africa, they revert in their advertising images to a set of tropes that Raymond Williams identified many years ago in *The Country and the City*, through which the beauty, civility and innocence of the big house in the country is upheld by wealthy denizens of the city who steadfastly overlook actual living conditions in the country. Thus, current real estate advertisements for farmland, country houses, and other exclusive

'reimagining South Africa is not easy when the material traces of symbolic power remain intact'

properties remain virtually unchanged in their symbolic and literal language from the 'Advertisement in a real estate agent's window' photographed by David Goldblatt in 1988. Above a caption reading 'A more perfect spot you will not find in the Natal Midlands than this superb smallholding with good views, water and a very desirable home', the advertisement seized on by Goldblatt features side-by-side images of the gracious thatched owner's house and the much plainer, more rundown outbuildings with farmworker, child (black) and dog in the foreground (Goldblatt, p54). Only a Martian could possibly imagine that the farmworker - or the dog - was actually the owner of the property photographed; to most viewers, however, the pictures suggest that the farm's goods and chattels *include* the farmworker and his child. Goldblatt's photograph thus draws attention to the ideological assumptions made by the original advertisers. What is remarkable is that more than ten years later real estate advertisements still rely on those familiar images of graciousness that obscure the violent economic system on which they depend, and still have the power to wipe actual spaces clean via the mystifying tradition of European pastoral representation. Indeed, in the free market of the free South Africa land redistribution has come to be as much about foreign opportunism and property speculation as it is about housing the homeless. The Western Cape, in particular, seems to be promoted on the international property market as a sort of California of the Southern hemisphere.

For example, while the present government is struggling admirably to deliver low-cost housing as promised to millions of its previously dispossessed citizens, South African Airways, the national airline, runs in-flight videos including reports of international beach volleyball and surfing competitions, as well as laudatory references to the snapping up of beautiful houses by 'the seriously wealthy'. One of the property advertisers in the typically glossy in-flight magazine - now sporting the suitably Africanised title *Sawubona* - is Hamptons International, whose South African affiliate, Pam Golding, sells exclusive properties in the Western Cape. Confirming Raymond Williams's insight that the country/city dynamic is reproduced in the colony/metropole dynamic, Ms Golding's very elaborate website is geared specifically to foreign investors looking for a second home in a beautiful setting.[5] Ms Golding's logo consists of a pair of highly elegant, cursive initials 'PG', flanking a pair of wrought iron gates hung on sturdy pillars - an image of exclusivity if ever there was one. In an informational 'Overview of the Western Cape', Golding lists the 'splendours of what we now know as the Cape Province' (never mind that that's nomenclature from the apartheid map). These splendours include the coastline, the scenery, the animal and plant life, prehistoric traces of 'the original San inhabitants' (some political correctness in that nomenclature) and the abundant leisure opportunities these features make possible. 'For many people', the 'Overview' concludes, 'the Cape Province is a special heaven, a place of spectacular beauty and excitement'. To enjoy the beauty and excitement of that special heaven, however, costs the 'many' a great deal of money. Meantime, on top of the massive unemployment and low wages which debar the poor from owning property, even for the middle classes mortgage interest rates as high as 25.5 per cent have meant that money has been hard to come by for rather more than many in South Africa. Hence the new removals of people from the rainbow nation, and hence the appeal to international buyers for whom a million rand, or even twenty, might not seem too steep a price to pay for 'A unique setting, surrounded by natural beauty-

---

5. Golding includes in her website a press-clipping dated December 1998 in which she is quoted as saying that her buyers are 'predominantly looking for retirement or second homes in South Africa because of the weather and outdoor lifestyle they can enjoy here'. For wealthy buyers from the northern hemisphere, a second home in South Africa offers the prospect of a kind of endless summer.

very private and very exclusive'.[6] The properties in Ms Golding's portfolio range from new developments with floorplans named 'Badger', 'Warbler', Moorhen', 'Nightjar' and so on (which allow the buyer to 'get a foot in the door of the soaring Cape property market'), through houses in 'the most exclusive private estate in Cape Town's City Bowl' (advertised with a photograph of a cricket match in progress), to the 20 million rand Rooshoek Wine Farm, claimed to be ideal not just for vines or olives but also 'as a corporate conference centre, country hotel, or guest farm'. Everywhere beneath the gushing pastoralisms, however, there is the subtext of crime in references to exclusivity, and remote-controlled security gates.

One property developer in the Cape has taken this pastoral/carceral idyll to its logical extreme. George Hazeldon last year broke ground on what Chris McGreal calls a 'modern version of a medieval walled city' near Somerset West some 25 miles east of Cape Town.[7] Heritage Park, as the development is called, will have churches, schools, shops, and lakes - even its own police force of about 40 men - all bounded by an electrified fence. Contrasting the lack of community in contemporary South African society with his own upbringing in a London, where 'you wouldn't do anything wrong because everyone knew you and they'd tell your mum and dad', Hazeldon imagines Heritage Park as a community complete unto itself, including graveyard and crematorium. Of course, given that this is the free South Africa, Heritage Park is not racially exclusive: says Hazeldon, 'The only criterion is that people want to live as good neighbours. We can build part of the rainbow nation here'. Not even walls and security gates, however, can hide what's really at the foot of the rainbow: the still-dispossessed South African poor. Hazeldon's way of dealing with the 1000-plus squatters living at the edge of Heritage Park is to build a township of 142 houses (working out at about 7 or 8 people per house) in the far corner of the development. They will be beyond the pale of the electric fence but Hazeldon expects some of the squatters to find work inside as maids or shop assistants. 'It's a win-win situation', says Hazeldon. 'They get free homes and we deal with an unsightly problem'. Indeed: we wouldn't like the view from

---

6. I first accessed Golding's web-site (at http://www.pamgolding.co.za) in April 1999. While the portfolio of properties has obviously changed, the rhetoric has not.
7. Chris McGreal, 'The Cape of Low Hopes', *Guardian Weekly*, 14 February 1999, p28. All quotes in this paragraph are from this article.

the top to be defiled, now, would we?

For those just coming as tourists to this post-apartheid South Africa where everyone wins, as might perhaps be expected, the emphasis on viewing natural beauty is even more striking. The blurb headed 'South Africa' in the Baobab Safari Company's lavishly printed brochure reads as follows:

> 'A world in one country' is South Africa's motto, and it's quite
> appropriate. Travel opportunities here are virtually unlimited and include
> superb wildlife safaris, beach holidays, mountain trekking, exciting
> modern cities, a fantasy-paradise resort casino and breathtaking scenery
> throughout. [Then here comes a little bit of history!] Through its
> extensive conservation efforts, South Africa has saved the white
> rhinoceros from extinction. [Are they talking about Eugene Terre
> Blanche?]

The double-page spread from which I have just taken this determinedly ahistorical quotation features: a gorgeous photograph, presumably taken from a helicopter or light aircraft, of lechwes fleeing across a vlei; a quotation from Henry Beston declaring that animals 'are not brethren, they are not underlings; they are other nations'; a black and white 'illustration of Zulu, 1889' (unnamed and uncredited) superimposed on drought-cracked mud; and a text provided by Beryl Markham, white settler aviatrix/author from 1930s Kenya, declaring, 'Africa is mystic; it is wild, it is a sweltering inferno, it is a photographer's paradise, an escapist's utopia; it is never dull'. As with that London publisher, the copywriters appear to have taken advantage of the end of apartheid not to make some sort of progressive, corrective re-writing of history but simply to make further capital out of exploitative images - in this case, of wild Africa and Africans.[8]

In fact, the end of apartheid seems to have exonerated the expensive tour operators of every last vestige of shame - finally they're free to advertise![9] If

---

8. While Baobab Safari Co sports a San Francisco address, their brochure carries the logo of three African airlines, Air Zimbabwe, South African Airways, and Kenya Airways.
9. For an intriguing look at local South African advertising in the wake of the first free elections in 1994, see Eve Bertelsen's article 'Ads and Amnesia: Black Advertising in the New South Africa', Nuttall and Coetzee, pp221-241.

Gap and Banana Republic fashions, Nissan Pathfinders, and Ralph Lauren paints can be sold by reference to the colonial safari experience, why not sell the original colonial safari experience by reference to the kind of class and luxury status ascribed to Gap and Banana Republic fashions, Nissan Pathfinders and Ralph Lauren paints. For $36,800 INTRAV offers you the chance to live the dream of the greatest African empire-builder of them all, Cecil Rhodes, going from Cape to Cairo in 22 days by 'Private Jet and the Legendary Blue Train'. Exclusive though this particular offer cracks itself up to be, its itinerary inviting you 'to discover the magic of Africa' turns out to be exactly the same as that offered by the Baobab people - Cape Town and its 'stunning backdrop' of Table Mountain, the wine farms, the game reserves, etc. etc.

The writers of these descriptions in these depressingly similar, apartheid-familiar brochures appear not to have made any effort to make use of the new histories coming out of South Africa. In the case of Cape Town, for instance, which Nigel Worden, Elizabeth van Heyningen and Vivian Bickford-Smith have chronicled in a wonderful synthesis of revisionist history and glossy packaging,[10] the brochures are still directing deep-pocketed tourists to the old VOC Castle, and even the 'famed Bushman exhibit at the South African Museum' (INTRAV brochure, p22) - the latter the subject of considerable revisionist controversy. Without any historical explanation, the INTRAV tour offers to take its clients to Paarl to view the Taal Monument, which, it says, regardless of the controversies surrounding both the monument and the language, 'represents the evolution of the Afrikaans language within South Africa'. With similar lack of contextualisation, the Maupin Tour invites its clients to 'enjoy a sightseeing excursion to the "Garden City" of Pretoria, displaying its Boer heritage', and includes a visit to the Voortrekker Monument which it simplistically describes as 'dedicated to the Boer settlers' victory over the Zulu' (Maupin brochure, p13). It fails to point out that the 'South Africa' referred to in that monument's cenotaph is the ethnically and racially exclusive one that allegedly passed away on Mandela's release; however, the Voortrekker monument still has dangerous separatist resonance, as indicated by David Goldblatt's May 1990 photograph of a Sunday service following a Conservative Party rally which

---

10. See *Cape Town: The Making of a City*, David Philip, Cape Town 1998; and *Cape Town in the Twentieth Century: An Illustrated Social History*, Human Rights Watch, London 2000.

used the monument as a backdrop for its banner calling for an '*eie toekoms*' [own/separate future] (Goldblatt, p175). As far as the brochure writers are concerned, however, the structure of things then is still unproblematically fodder for sightseeing now.

Meanwhile tourist ephemera such as postcards remain virtually identical to those produced in the apartheid era, if slightly glossier. Even the declaration of Robben Island as a UN-designated world heritage site and its opening as a tourist destination for visitors to Cape Town (whether presidents or ordinary citizens) is curious. This strangely photogenic site is neither the equivalent of Alcatraz (having been overtly political) nor of Auschwitz (not being a death camp). In fact, therefore, the new prison-as-tourist-site, while apparently making visible what used to be invisible - and flight-paths around Cape Town have now been altered so that planes routinely overfly the formerly forbidden space - can almost be seen as a re-sanitation of apartheid. This was a place Mandela survived, after all, the legendary 'Mandela U'. Indeed, in his autobiography, Mandela begins his second section on life on Robben Island, entitled 'Beginning to Hope', with references to improving prison conditions:

> We had won a host of small battles that added up to a change
> in the atmosphere of the island. While we did not run it, the authorities
> could not run it without us, and in the aftermath of [Warden] van
> Rensburg's departure, our life became more tolerable.[11]

In the illustrated version of the autobiography, a sombre photograph of veteran ANC leader Walter Sisulu bears the following wry caption: 'Walter Sisulu on a return visit to the lime quarry where he taught political history to his fellow-prisoners'.[12]

In ironically subverting the notion of apartheid control and power, these verbal and visual images share two important features of much of the various oral history projects pioneered by Charles van Onselen in the 1980s.[13] They are important psychologically in asserting that apartheid was never successful in

---

11. Nelson Mandela, *Long Walk to Freedom*, Abacus, London, 1995, p535.
12. Nelson Mandela, *Mandela: An Illustrated Autobiography*, Little, Brown, and Co, Boston 1996, p139.

breaking the spirit of the people it imprisoned, and, intellectually, in deconstructing the spectacular machinery of state power - by which I mean that they reveal that at the ordinary level of interaction between individual blacks - whether 'unknown' figures like the share-cropper Kas Maine, or political figures like Mandela or Sisulu - and individual whites, questions of power were not as clear-cut as they might have seemed. However, while I recognise the deconstructive value of these images and the oral histories, and see them as potentially useful in thinking about past, present, and future, making the physical structure of Robben Island into a tourist venue as a material analogue of the institutional structures of apartheid, seems in some ways to evade the great blank spaces of still-repressed memory in South Africa. For, while life on Robben Island may have been hard and cruel, the prison nonetheless represents, among other things, the weird legalism of apartheid, recordable, recoverable, and capable of revision and subversion. The grossest of apartheid atrocities, meanwhile, were perpetrated extra-legally in spaces which permit no irony, and their perpetrators took care to leave no traces: they burned the bodies, they shredded the documents.

For many foreigners - gentlemen-pornographers, businessmen, tourists and property-buyers alike - no doubt these concerns won't be significant - they will merely be happy to remain in gated luxury, secure from other people's criminal attacks on them, grateful to the new order for absolving them of any guilt by complicity; but when they have photographed the visual marks of the severely restricted version of South African history that is presented to them, will they consider, as they return from the unexplored empty spaces of the hinterland, that the real magic of Africa might be in making the savagery of white rule vanish from sight?

---

13. See for instance van Onselen's award-winning *The Seed is Mine: The Life of Kas Maine, a South African Sharecropper 1894-1985*, David Philip, Cape Town 1996.

Disintegrative pressure and the sociology of disintegration

Review article by Tom Wengraf

Pierre Bourdieu et al, *The Weight of the World: social suffering in contemporary society*, Polity Press 1999

My response to this work goes through two repeating phases: great personal interest in the variety of social experiences vividly described and suggested in the fifty or so interviews transcribed and/or commented upon; followed by mounting irritation with it as a work of sociological research; and then the cycle starts again. This review of the book is in part an attempt to understand this confusing double reaction.

One of the few French (or Continental European) sociologists known to the anglophone sociological community, Pierre Bourdieu has been doing pioneering and illuminating social research on his own and in teams for over forty years.

In 1993, he and some twenty collaborators published *La misére du monde* (Seuil 1993 - MM in this text); *The Weight of the World* (WW) is a shortened version of this, which has just been published in English. MM has had great success in France at a popular level, triggering a wide-ranging public debate on inequality, politics and civic solidarity, even generating plays for the theatre in Paris. Social work professionals have seized on it as a way of coming to terms with many of the changes affecting their clients. Activists have found documentation for a sharper understanding of the impact on the lives and situations of ordinary people as the drive to domination of global corporations has decomposed the social order of the 1945-1975 period in France as in the UK. In terms of the political purposes identified in the 'post-script', the work has been a definite political success. Composed primarily of vivid interviews (and commentaries on those interviews) with people at or near the bottom of the social pile, the book is powerfully evocative of a myriad of social milieux, a cluster of uncomprehending generations; it also captures a sense of the strong tendencies fostering the disintegration of bonds of trust and mutuality within and between social categories, in the public, private and social spheres.

Although the book, deservedly, appeals to a wide public in France - and I hope that this edition will now do so in anglophone countries - some social scientists have condemned it as professionally unacceptable. This also needs to be understood. Is the book being 'snubbed' by envious sociologists because it is so popular? Or is it so popular because - within a frame provided by the prestige of science in general and the reputation of Bourdieu in particular - it is scientifically and conceptually so undemanding? Or do we need a more complex explanation? This review will explore some of these issues.

Between one-half and two-thirds of *WW* is composed of some 50 interviews (60 in MM), selected from the original 182 gathered over three years. They are surrounded by other texts - commentaries, with theoretical and methodological discussions, statistical data, personal documents etc.

Commentaries and transcripts

The reader is given only the briefest of introductions to the material. A working philosophy (on which we shall comment later) is set out:

> Although these interviews were conceived and constructed as self-sufficient wholes, and can be read separately (and in any order), the reading has been set up to bring together individuals in social categories that might well be found together … We hope that this structure will have two effects. It should become clear that so-called 'difficult' spots ('housing projects' or schools today) are … difficult to describe and think about … Second, following the lead of novelists such as Faulkner, Joyce or Woolf, we must relinquish the single, central, dominant, in a word, quasi-divine point of view that is all too

easily adopted by observers - and by readers too. We must work instead with the multiple perspectives that correspond to the multiplicity of coexisting, and sometimes directly competing, points of view (p3).

The reader then plunges into the main body of the 50 interviews, which are aggregated into some six sections of rather unequal length. A brief account of these 'sections' is given below.

The space of points of view

There is a principle operating of the 'juxtaposition' of accounts from people who might find themselves confronting each other in roughly the same physical space: for example, shopkeepers and vandalising and stealing youths; the superintendents or custodians of council flats and the tenants; adults and adolescents; quiet families and noisy families; immigrant families and anti-immigrant families, proletarians and subproletarians, etc.

Through accounts of routine deteriorations and sudden clashes, daily lives are evoked - of life in big city low-income housing suburbs, where the inhabitants are separated by differences of generation, culture and social milieu, but are forced to cohabit and/or work together and so antagonise each other in the irritations of everyday living. Abdelmalek Sayad's juxtaposition of interviews with the Ben Miloud family and with Mme Meunier who lives next door is eloquent of the deep vulnerabilities, antagonisms and furies raised.

The effects of place

We are then transported to the US inner cities, because, as Wacquant puts it (in his essay 'America as social dystopia: the politics of urban disintegration, or, The French Uses of the 'American Model'):

> by treating America's dark ghetto as a sociological blueprint … we may form a picture of the effects that could eventually result from the radicalisation of certain processes of dualisation now incipient in disadvantaged French neighbourhoods. Like a magnifying glass that also deforms what it shows, the American ghetto gives us a realistic vision of the kind of relationships likely to develop when the State jettisons its essential mission to sustain the organisational infrastructure indispensable to the functioning of any complex

urban society, pursues a policy of systematic erosion of public institutions, and gives in to market forces … If, owing to their technocratic myopias and fascinated fixation on short-term financial performance, France's ruling elites of both left and right persist with the neoconservative policy of 'downsizing' the public sector and rampant commodification of social relations they have pursued since the mid-seventies, then one cannot rule out that what is today still a distant and frightful dystopia might one day turn into an all too close and familiar reality (pp132-9).

Two interviews then follow with a black hustler in Chicago and with a Puerto Rican in Spanish Harlem, 'Homeless in El Barrio'.

The abdication of the state

This section identifies the neo-liberal turn of the state as the primary cause of problems of daily life, in its notion of the decline of the public services and the idea of the public. (The abdication by owners and managers of corporate capital from any social responsibility, or taxation, to compensate for the effects of their practices and policies at a local or a world level is taken for granted in the text.) The section explores the specific points-of-view of lower agents of the neo-liberalising state (social workers, police and justice professionals), who lack the resources to tackle the growing daily problems of populations increasingly abandoned as political elites and higher state officials seek corporate benefits in the erosion and privatisation of the state. A particularly powerful interview in this section is 'Mission Impossible', an interview with Pascale R, a project head for urban revitalisation projects. Her interview illuminates the predicaments of alleged 'change agents', through her experience in two different projects, and two different histories of the ways in which her mission to increase participation and co-ordination got terminated or blocked. As Bourdieu remarks in his introduction to the transcript:

> In T, where she had real power over one of the factors of the problem she had to deal with - housing - she was able to push her work far enough to reveal the profoundly contradictory base of the mission that she had been assigned. In F, where she is left to her own devices, that is to say to the purely symbolic devices of conviction and persuasion, she is discovering right from the start

that she is unable to give the things that people want and can only offer things they do not want (like the 'traineeships' that are makeshift remedies for unemployment). What could really change the situation that she is being asked to change does not depend on her, whereas what does depend on her cannot really change anything (p190).

The same 'institutional bad faith', in which impossible missions are given, necessary resources are denied and 'awkward people' are removed, can be found in the summary of interviews with Denis J, a sentencing magistrate, with Francis T, a 'street educator' dealing with people on hard drugs ('avant-garde for an institution to which he offers irreplaceable services but which is always ready to disown him'); they are also found in Lenoir's mini-section, 'Disorder among the Agents of Order', in interviews with a policewoman and with a judge. The agents of the state interviewed here are 'awkward figures', who take the official ideologies of their institutions so seriously that they endanger the institutional bad faith and dishonesty on which the real practice of state power depends. Their unsatisfactory experiences - and those of other 'agents', especially from the educational sphere - provide acute insight into the operations and milieux in which they are involved.

On the way down

This is another very good section, to my mind the best in the book; it addresses the consequences of the transformations that have taken place in the labour market, the effects of the casualisation of work and the worsening conditions for the working classes in industry, in agriculture, in small enterprises and in office work. The decline of solidarities and disillusion with parties and unions contribute to this demoralisation and to the precariousness of the world of labour and what appears as a 'past' world of labour movements and solidarities. The titles of particular interviews convey the sense of this: 'Hanging by a thread' (an interview with a woman out of work), and 'Such a fragile equilibrium' (a joint interview with a Portuguese couple, who have discovered the absence of official or informal support in the face of any occurrence (loss of a job, an illness) that throws their insecure fragile 'security' into question: they painfully discover that people, and institutions, and French society 'don't want to know'). Pialoux's understanding of the new structural tendencies and management strategies -

that produce 'The Shop Steward's World in Disarray' - is based on long and intimate knowledge of an evolving and recomposing 'world of work and meanings'. He has produced a brilliant evocation of the uncomprehending struggle and generation/epochal gap between the older activist 'permanent workers' and the younger world of adaptive individual 'temps' struggling to be acceptable to managements. Sandrine Garcia's 'The Stolen Work' evokes class and power struggles within the feminist movement, and Rosine Christin contributes very telling portrayals of women in the workforce. It's worth getting a copy of *Weight of the World* just for the analyses and transcripts in this section alone (pp255-420).

Outcasts on the inside

This is a section where teachers and young people, especially in sixth-form and technical colleges, express their perspectives; it shows the perverse effects of a policy which tries to bring 80 per cent of the age-grade to the 'bac' - the equivalent of A-levels - but only offers, for lack of additional per capita resources, a devalorised qualification, and a school not adapted to them, and at the same time raises expectations that are not going to be satisfied. For some this produces mild demoralisation (Broccolichi's 'Paradise Lost' interview with three high school students); for others, it produces a world of perpetual insult, and attempted moral and physical attacks, by (ex) students and by parents, on teachers and schools. In this 'universe', any hope that lives might be improved by education is either denied or expressed as chronic rage, as is shown in 'Institutional Violence', an interview with a junior high school principal in an Educational Priority Zone (pp492-506). In this area, the 'American dystopia' has already fully arrived, as it has also in large parts of the UK.

The contradictions of inheritance

This 'betrayal by the state through the schools' (betrayal both of teachers and of the families of children) leads on to the last section which focuses on 'the family' as a place of contradictory injunctions, where the worlds of parents and of children are torn apart and confront each other, especially in the case of immigrant families. Social suffering is most strongly expressed there, as frustrated upward and forced downward mobilities impinge. There is a greater representation here than in some other sections of middle classes under pressure:

the film editor whose situation is explored in 'Wife and Colleague', and Sebastien K, a political journalist for a radio station. An account which happens to be placed in the work section could be placed here: Bourdieu's 'A Life Lost', expressing the inarticulate suffering of a farmer, the meaning of whose very arduous life is destroyed when his son refuses to take over the farm.

Evaluation

How does the text make sense of these often heart-breaking and socially-enraging cases? It is here that I start to feel reservations and frustrations.

There is no proper overview of the structure of the book as a whole. You get closest to one by looking at the contents pages, but the titles of the interviews are allusive and literary, giving no clear guide to the type of person being interviewed or their (pseudonymous) name. The failure of the chapter titles to specify the social category from which an interviewee is drawn, as well as the absence of any discursive overviews, makes it as difficult as possible for the reader to find or retrieve interviews appropriate for different research purposes. There are introductions to each of the main sections, but these sociological-general essays by Bourdieu, with or without a collaborator, are much too general. They could have been written before the gathering of the interview data or their writing-up.

There is therefore a yawning gap between the general (these introductions and the long methodological essay on 'Understanding' at the back of the book) and the study of the particular cases, each one of which is treated separately. Even where two or three successive interviews are by the same researcher, the most frequent pattern is that each interview is introduced separately. At one point, Champagne writes on 'The View from the State', followed by Sayad on 'The "costs" and "benefits" of immigration'. Lenoir then writes a good general essay on 'Disorder among the Agents of Order' before writing an introduction and transcript based on his interview with Agnes ('Woman and Cop') and then another ('A living reproach') about a judge, Andre S. But none of the three non-transcript pieces refer to any of the others. As a result, the reader has to do all the work of making coherent sense of these five components of what appears typographically to be a mini-section.

To me it feels as if the book is constructed to avoid any comparative theorising based on, and attentive to, case material: either you run with the super-generalities, or you are lost in the particularities in each case. No rationale is given for this 'individualising' construction: if the idea was to let the reader engage in the comparative theorising, then this is blocked by the fact that the 'commentary on each transcript' comes before the transcript, thus preventing the reader from making a different sense of the interview material from that provided in advance by the commentary. Consequently the reader's own emergent understanding or theorising is blocked, or at least rendered extremely difficult, while the social researchers responsible for the presentation (if they have such a coherent perspective) conceal it completely.

Some understanding of this peculiar construction is suggested by the 'postscript'. This explains the book's political purpose: to enable middle-class and elite readers 'up there' to become aware of the thoughts and sufferings of 'those below', the masses of little people, so as to interrupt the self-preoccupation of elites concerned only with themselves and their internal rivalries. Such forcing of the raw suffering of 'little people' into public discourse could be taken as the equivalent in Britain of some fifty *Cathy Come Homes*.

In this sense, the nature of the book comes into focus. It is not aimed at sociologists and social researchers but primarily at the 'middle-class elite' of general readers, more likely to be emotionally and politically unsettled by individual hard cases and sharp commentary upon them (reading transcript and commentary one at a time) than they are by the drudgery of social science theorising.

The result is a very valuable source/resource book of mostly good interviews, which firmly resists any coherent and differentiated analysis or understanding. The particularities are too particular, the theorisations and commentary are too abstract.

However, the difficulty of doing more than 'dipping' into cases will be felt not only by the would-be theorising social researcher (how does this case, these Z numbers of cases, advance our understanding of X?) but also by the ordinary common reader; the weight of detail and number of stories finally defeats any attempt to 'draw lessons', except the simplest namely 'what a lot of suffering there is!' The danger is that of inducing *in any reader* 'compassion fatigue', in which the weight of all this misery in the end produces a type of 'burn-out' of sympathy. An early rise in indignation is followed by a longer period of fatalist acceptance as one miserable story follows another, and no 'theoretical insight' is generated or developed.[1]

Doubts about the social-science contribution of the work as a whole are if anything amplified by the edition's enthusiastic introduction by the North American translator, who argues that a feature of *The Weight of the World* is 'its exploration of a decidedly French setting even as it claims a significance that transcends any particular setting'. As it transpires, in her introduction differences between North America and Europe, between the USA and France, are denied, through the use of the transatlantic-universalist term of 'contemporary society'. The translator-in-chief, from Columbia University, celebrates the fact that the 'narratives' have 'worked well' for her in her courses in sociology. She argues that

> Many readers will read these interviews as short stories - windows on contemporary society opened by narratives about how that society is experienced by individuals from many walks of life and social situations. And indeed these narratives are quite wonderful. (They have worked well for me in my courses in sociology.) The translator's goal with the interview as story must be to render the quality of these diverse lives, the pungency, the pathos, as the case may be, and the specificity of their social and work settings (the automobile plant, the school system, the political landscape, and so on).

(It could also be noted that the 'settings' described here are in the nationally unspecific generic landscapes of that same 'contemporary society'.) It is not clear from this whether theoretical insightfulness is considered as important as the expressive qualities of the 'short stories'. It is not clear that reading 'narratives showing how contemporary society is experienced' actually involves showing how sociological researchers 'understand' and theorise such 'experiencing', in a way *which goes beyond merely recycling* the experiencing of those involved.

Bourdieu's introductory note to the reader comprises less than 2 pages (for a work of over 600 pages in the Anglo edition, 1000 in the 1993 French edition): this suggests a bad conscience. He writes that some will consider the 'case studies'

---

1. The elimination in the 'Anglo' edition of a group discussion with three militants of the French Socialist Party, and of an interview with a deputy mayor who 'dreams of another 1789', enhances this effect of the apparent elimination of any 'political' potential.

as so many different short stories, and asks how we can avoid making the interview and its analytic prologue look like a clinical case preceded by a diagnosis. The answer has to be: *not in the way it is presented in this book*. The book makes a certain sort of reading almost inevitable: and then warns the reader against taking the text in the way that the structure of the book makes overwhelmingly probable.

Normally, a sociological enterprise will define its conceptual framework and the central research questions; it will identify a research design appropriate for those research questions with a sampling procedure for obtaining theoretically-relevant data, and an analytic procedure for 'interpreting' the data obtained; it will end with a conclusion about the relevance of the interpreted data to the research questions that defined the inquiry.

None of this happens in this presentation. The sampling principles are not specified. As one of the book's critics asks, quite pertinently, 'Why privilege the suburb and the school, rather than prisons, military camps and the asylums? Why interview teachers but not the nurses, agriculturists but not fishermen and lorry-drivers, handicapped people but not people HIV-positive?[2] People are interviewed from a very wide range of social categories, but the principles for the selection of categories and of people in them are not made explicit.

This failure to specify the principles of the sample goes together with a failure to specify the apparent central concept of the inquiry - '*la misére*' in the original, 'suffering' in English. This concept does not even make it into the title of the English edition; and in the index it has only one page reference!

Similarly, there is a considerable discussion of abstract principles of interviewing in the end-essay, 'Understanding', but no guidance as to how the interviews were carried out, or how these principles were used to guide the large number of interviewers who ranged from the professional to the amateur. The impression given from glancing through the transcripts is that no common schedule of themes or initial questions was used.

Also jettisoned is any clarification of the procedures for the analysis of the interview material; the drawing of conclusions in terms of an organising research

---

2. N. Mayer, 'L'entretien selon Pierre Bourdieu: analyse critique de *La misére du monde*', *Revue française de sociologie* 1996, p359.

question or *problématique*; or the production of a report systematically making clear to the reader the research design, implementation and reporting.

Bourdieu's critical-theoretical sociology (1968 specification) against common-sense

Bourdieu's earlier research was devoted to understanding actors differently from the way the local culture allows them to understand themselves.[3] This earlier position was that held by a very large body of anti-positivist, anti-empiricist, social researchers, in France stemming from the work of Durkheim, but reinforced by a parallel critique by Marxist social science of the ideological illusions of local common-sense and common-sense appearances. In the philosophy of science, Gaston Bachelard had laid the epistemological bases for science (both the natural and the social varieties) as requiring and being based upon the constant critique of common-sense pre-scientific notions and concepts.[4] Sociology, like science in general, was consequently unlikely to be popular, precisely because it was a practice of critiquing and 'deconstructing' the local ideologies and false consciousness and common-sense in which 'immediate experience' plunged social actors. It was a demystification.

Although this position is to be found dotted about the text of *WW*, the 'working philosophy' of the book, cited at the start of this review, goes quite against it. The value added by the sociologist typically does not involve treating points of view as self-sufficient or self-explanatory wholes; it does not involve considering that evidence from 50 or 150 interviews can be read 'in any order'. Perspectives are not their own explanation. The value added by the sociologist lies in 'working with multiple perspectives' to produce an emergent point of view which helps to make sense of the others. That emergent 'view from somewhere else' is what the sociologist is there to provide (the comparative and theorising sociologist, as opposed to the editor, who simply juxtaposes self-sufficient interviews to be read in any order).

Such a position is articulated in a number of places in *WW*, for example in a critique of media information overload by Patrick Champagne:

---

3. See P. Bourdieu, J.-C. Chamboredon, and J.-C. Passeron, *Le métier du sociologue*, Mouton-Bordas, Paris 1968.
4. G. Bachelard, *La formation de l'esprit scientifique*, Vrin, Paris 1999.

The overabundance of miscellaneous news and analyses generates confusion and leaves the field open to partial or illusory explanations. From then on, each person can easily find the explanations they want to hear ... The principal task for sociology, and not the easiest one, is to distinguish between what is relevant and what is less so, between what is important and what is only secondary or derivative. Sociology must above all hierarchise and integrate in a coherent explanatory system a collection of factors that are far from all having the same functional weight (p214).

It is also strongly present in the end-essay 'Understanding', and in the political 'postscript'. However, for the most part the text of WW starts, and in practice for the ordinary reader stays, with the 'lived experience' of the different social actors who tell the truth of their social suffering directly to the reader.

1993 Politico-sociological defeatism: corporate differences and contradictions rule, OK!

Small wonder, therefore, that sociologists have felt unsympathetic with this ignoring and transgressing of the 'scientificity' of their normative model; many of them will have learnt such a model from the work and example of Bourdieu himself!

Within the implicit conceptual-interpretive framework, there are shifts which are worth mentioning: away from the concepts of 'class' and of 'cultural and economic capitals' so characteristic of Bourdieu's early work, and towards an implicitly 'eternalised' model of 'social hierarchy'.[5]

The 'defeatism' of the older generation of shop stewards so well described in 'On the Way Down' finds its correlate in the implicit meta-narrative of the constructed text, and the absence of theory in WW (representing the defeated intellectual shop stewards of those oppressed in the class structure and social hierarchy?).[6] The defeatism of Bourdieu's juxtapositionism of the space of 'points-of-view' is based on the unstated assumption that none of the separate social categories can be brought together in a collective solidarity that can transcend

---

5. This is discussed in another critique: G. Grundberg and E. Schweissguth, 'Bourdieu at la misére: une approache reductionniste', *Revue français de la science politique* 1996.
6. The Anglo edition accentuates this in a number of ways, for example by omitting the discussion with Socialist Party activists - see note 1.

their corporate differences. The points of view cannot be reconciled. There is no sense of a counter-hegemonic possibility: no sense that a political party (such as the former French Communist Party) or any community collectivist movement could create any sort of mutual understanding or 'rainbow coalition'. Indeed, the opposite: Bourdieu is categorical:

> It is within each of these permanent groups (neighbours or co-workers) which set the lived boundary for all their experiences, that the oppositions (especially salient where lifestyle is concerned) separating classes, ethnic groups or generations, are perceived and experienced - with all the misperceptions this entails. Bringing together individuals who otherwise have nothing in common, especially where they live or work, only exacerbates the conflict (p4) [I have reversed the order of the two sentences].[7]

The implication is quite clear that a preferable policy would be one which kept such classes, ethnic groups, and generations - groups who have nothing in common, it seems - firmly apart from each other. A despairing call for a complex system of sociological apartheid is the - no doubt unconscious - implication of this collusive recycling of their (and perhaps the defeatist readers') common-sense.

Simply staying with and recycling the actor's told story and their self-theory, the illusions of their common-sense as Bourdieu might previously have put it, is scientifically and politically regressive.

Explanations: populist and critical-theoretical sociology and their tensions

Let us now consider how this might have come about.

Perhaps Bourdieu is performing a *covert operation*? A coherent theoretical-ideological project which dare not say its name? It might be that Bourdieu is

---

7. A quite different approach was used in another large-scale biographic project with which I was involved, Social Strategies in Risk Societies. In this project some 250 life history interviews were conducted, in France and six other European countries (see P.M. Chamberlayne & M.J. Rustin, *From Biography to Social Policy: Final Report of Sostris Project*, Centre for Biography in Social Policy, University of East London; for a discussion of the project's approach to biographical material see my essay in the report, 'Uncovering the general from within the particular: from contingencies to typologies in the understanding of cases').

engaged in a covert struggle against local common-sense feelings through his device of 'sympathetic juxtaposition'. This seems unlikely.

Perhaps it is an experiment in theoretically incoherent experiential empathy -sociology for political purposes? Has Bourdieu stepped outside the 'unpopular and alienating' science of sociology - while lending the project his prestige and the prestige of sociology - to insist on the suffering induced by further developments of the capitalist mode of production, even at the cost of professional self-discreditation? Discharging a personal-political responsibility at the cost of not advancing social science?

This seems likely to me - Mayer, for example, in her critical review of the book, puts forward the 'political' dimension of the project as one with which she does not, as a sociologist, concern herself.[8]

A question then arises however: what is it, then, about the dominant modes of mainstream (French) sociology of a theoretical and objectivist sort that makes it necessary to 'put it aside' to have a full political impact? This returns us to the question of the 'adequacy of sociology', or at least of the critical-theoretical sociology with which Bourdieu was previously associated and for which people like myself have admired him.

Have (French) sociologists - like the elites of (French) society - become completely introspective and out-of-contact with the suffering of ordinary poor people? In England, it could be argued that sociologists have in the main over the last thirty years become less in contact with popular movements for change and more engaged in more internal disputes of an increasingly trivial and arcane sort. If the same thing has happened in France, then this would explain why Bourdieu's covert target in the 'political postscript' (whether conscious or unconscious) may be the increasing irrelevance of elite sociology to mass misery and movements for change. In such a case, any attempt to 'recontact' and rediscover awareness of the non-affluence of the affluent societies is likely to be salutary.

However, such a 'rediscovery of poverty' (similar to the left-wing critique in the late 1950s and 1960s of the US-dominated academic sociology of the 1945-55 Cold War period) will be weak in its effect if it operates in such a fashion as to apparently confirm the 'sense of hopelessness and inevitability' that most of

---

8. See note 2.

those studied express and that the 'commentaries' by and large recycle.

And this is what appears to happen: presenting and recycling the told story and the 'morals of the story' expressed and communicated by the interviewees in WW seems to confirm for the reader that the fears of the interviewees are only too justified and their hopes for improvement are only too illusory. The commentaries if anything increase the reader's sense of the absurdity of hope and hence of 'the necessity of despair'. The elimination in the 'Anglo' edition of interviews with 'politicos' seems likely to enhance this effect.

However, there is a cost to doing the opposite - *not* staying close to and identified with the experience of 'a suffering whose truth is spoken, here, by those who live it' (French pocket edition, back cover). And this cost is that the relatively detached, relatively contextualising, perhaps even relatively ironic view of the sociologist, who makes a different sense from that which is made by the actor, and tells a truth different from the truth articulated by the sufferer, leads to an emotional alienation of the reader from the actor-sufferer. Seeing through the eyes of the sociologist-writer, the reader sees more and sees through, but does not experience with, the actor-sufferer.

It can often appear as a zero-sum game: the more sociological understanding, the less emotional impact of the person reported upon; the more truth of the person and their perspective, the less sociological understanding. Finding a mode of conveying the different truths of the researcher without reducing the emotional empathy of the reader for the interviewee is exceedingly difficult. The text of this book is struggling with this problem.

There is also the question of a lack of a historical sociological imagination. Neither Bourdieu nor his American translator situate the 'researched moment' in which the interviews took place and were 'commented upon'. The 'Anglo reader' of the year 2000 not only loses the specificity of French as opposed to non-French societies, but also is given no historical range of the specific historical moment in which the interviews were undertaken and the commentaries and introductions written. The banal concept of contemporary society indicates a vacuous and vacated sense of time.

It might be worth considering whether the end of the 1980s and the beginning of the 1990s were a particularly bad time both for left-wing French sociology and for popular milieux in France. This may make the homology between the told stories of the interviewees and the implicit and explicit metanarratives of the sociologists more explicable.

Such are the many issues posed both by the procedure and substance of the research work that went into the *Weight of the World* and by its method of presentation and commentary

Conclusion

There is a permanent tension in social research between the detailed study of particular cases and the attempt to theorise by comparative study the implications of such particular research. C. Wright Mills, in his *Sociological Imagination* published in 1960, was already discussing the way bad sociology took the form of dividing itself into three degenerate traditions: abstracted theorising; empiricist plunges into the details of particular cases; and a methodological discourse intrinsically separate from both. Despite the presence and frequency of desperate warnings against such practices in WW, we find unfortunately that they are to some extent reproduced.

An important question of evolving historical context might be adduced as a part explanation. At certain moments in history, at particular locations in particular societies, the politically most urgent priority for left-wing sociologists writing for their publics will be to engage in a critique of false happy consciousness: in times of considerable prosperity, consciousness critique by way of Freud or Marx or feminism may be crucial. Yes, people are superficially happy, but we need to have a critique of happy materialism. At other moments, in other locations, the deterioration of material conditions may mean that the politically most urgent task is to document for targeted sociological publics that deterioration of conditions, to make sure that ignorance is subverted by relatively straightforward knowledge. MM would then be an index of the degree of middle-class ignorance of conditions at the bottom of an intensifying social hierarchy.

But despite its overall implicit theoretical weakness and its presentational incoherence and the fact that it cannot be read as a whole or used as a model of social-science research, the text is a considerable achievement as a source-book and as a resource for understanding French and other societies, especially those likewise struggling against the neo-liberal orthodoxy of power. WW's evocation of milieux and popular experience at a particular moment of French history (late 1980s, early 1990s) is unparalleled; and as a populist spin-off from sociology it suggests powerful and political lessons (not only in France but also in the UK and elsewhere) for all those concerned - as participants, activists or researchers - with the struggles of the current epoch, as we increasingly struggle to understand and resist the effects of the intensifying irresponsibility of 'global money powers'.

British readers may recall the precedent of Goldthorpe and Lockwood's *The Affluent Worker* (reprinted by CUP in 1996): its publication was followed by the labour unrest and labour movement action that the book had predicted as gone for good. Similarly, France in the later 1990s seemed much more promising than the France of these interviews. As a source of action-enflaming understanding, this translation of Bourdieu's work might have a definite contribution to make in the UK.

Brave new families?
Rosalind Delmar

Helen Wilkinson (ed), *Family Business*, Demos £9.95

On all sides we hear that the family is in flux and turmoil, with new household arrangements, a declining birth rate, the unpopularity of marriage and the crisis in sex roles initiated by increasing gender equality invoked as symptoms and as causes. Add to this brave new world scenarios of cloning and other new reproductive technologies, increasing commodification of sexuality and the worship of transnational corporations, and we can all wonder where the future lies. Will all this lead to the death of the family and its replacement by reproduction units? Will the family wither away, or change its form?

A segment of the debate is set out in *Family Business*. It gives us a chance to look at the range of ideas which inform current thinking on the centre left, from a perspective which in general supports government policy – aimed at the creation of a new worker-parent citizen, whose family responsibilities are shared not just with their life-partner or other family members but with government and employer too. As such it is a handy volume. Interestingly enough, whilst the arguments are often couched in the language of economic rationalism, they reveal a strong idealism.

The central question is this: given that the family is still the basic unit of civil society, how should government, global/corporate capitalist enterprises and citizens combine in partnership to produce a family form suitable for the needs of all?

The articles signalled as most important in the book, coming from the 'global intellectual family' of its editor (p3), adopt a neo-feminist approach, combining a commitment to equality in workplace and home with a desire that the economic function of the family should be made central to its definition. In this way the family will take its place within the global market place rather than remaining marginal and therefore reactive. 'In a world that commodifies our time and attention more than ever before', argues Wilkinson, 'families must be properly valued in economic, as well as moral, terms' (p20). This economic function is to 'create nurture and sustain society's present and future "human capital"', writes Arlene Skolnick (p32). Ed Straw explores the family as skills agency and learning centre (p135). Shirley Burggraf calls for a new social contract which would recognise the economic value of the work families do and make parents 'shareholders in their own families', through the privatisation of social insurance so that those with children are not expected to support the childless (p38). Thus the family is defined as a unit for the production and reproduction of human resources, a classic small producer, which needs financing as such. Given global companies' need for a flexible and skilled workforce and the crucial position occupied by families in producing these human resources, it is, so the argument goes, in the best interests of government and capital to support effective families. It is 'in the national interest to invest in parenting and family life' (Wilkinson, p20). In this way globalisation need not necessarily generate the economic insecurity which has seemed its hallmark up to now.

In a keynote article, the current director of Demos, Tom Bentley, extends the metaphor of the 'family business'. At its core are parents and children, committed to 'strong relationships' and 'carefully balanced career planning', bolstered by 'associates' who may help with babysitting and other kinds of child care (and may expect personal involvement in return), and then subcontractors, nannies, caterers, 'supply mums and dads'. These are networking families with clear objectives from the outset, and their outlook is that of a rational economic subject. What is excluded from his picture (and from the book in general) are situations and events which can deal devastating blows to even the most forward-looking. Most striking is the absence of any discussion of health, physical or mental. Only Ian Christie's article considers housing, one of the most important policy areas for families. Also unmentioned is unemployment. Yet it casts its shadow over the book. What else but the fear of unemployment and its consequences, vividly felt after almost two decades of redundancies, dependence on short term contracts and other ills, can explain such eagerness to introduce the cash nexus into family relationships? Why else should the single most important criterion employed here to evaluate parenting and co-parenting arrangements be whether they will help a parent get to work on time and develop and maintain a career?

The underlying wish is for a utopian outcome: to emerge from a period of turbulence, upheaval and uncertainty into a state of harmonious fit not just between business, government and citizens, but within each sector too. There is more than a touch of idealism in the belief that an appropriate family form can be engineered by social policy or that the actors in the global marketplace will recognise that what is best for their employees is best for them.

If the language of the small business applied to the family opens up a prospect of economic security for all, what is it that is taken away? As Michael Rustin points out in his article, what is lost is affect, the emotional exchanges which are the stuff of family life, and which are conducted by the rules of gift and barter rather than those of the market place (p69). These are impossible to integrate within a monetary system and yet crucial in the processes of socialisation and acculturation. This is the article which most clearly denounces the government's insistence that single mothers of small children in receipt of state benefit should find work, and most clearly argues for an active welfare approach to family need.

However, the only contribution which directly addresses 'human nature' comes from the Darwinists Helena Cronin and Oliver Curry, who link family breakdown to male unemployment (which makes men less desirable marriage partners), and to gender equality, which, they claim, flies in the face of the basic law that women will always want mates who are of higher status and earning power. This further restricts the pool from which women can choose. Until the balance is got right, they claim, the myth will be perpetuated by 'parasitic counsellors and well-meaning commentators' that the problems created by inequality and disadvantage 'can be erased in a few therapy sessions'(p157). So much for *Relate* and other counselling services. If the government focuses on creating male employment and recognises that women have different needs and preferences from men, a happier state of affairs will be ushered in.

What they don't make clear is on what basis they can claim to be dealing with universal laws rather than statistical frequencies. (It would be interesting to know whether they apply these laws to their own work, and support on principle salary differentials for male and female academics.) In fact their employment of universal categories is unhelpful and sloppy. They fail to differentiate between the various sets of interests and needs of different groups of women, and at different points in their lives. Thus 'following the birth of the first child, women work less, men work more' (p157). Such universalising statements are worse than useless at a time when childlessness has become a meaningful option. It is inadequate to limit all women's potentialities on the grounds that some will choose to have children and would then prefer to spend part of their lives putting maternity first. Moreover, there will be times and occasions where the interests of women who are not mothers and those who are will and do collide: the recent survey which demonstrated resentment by the childless aroused by 'family friendly' policies at work is one small example.

It is significant that the dominant function of the family in *Family Business* is the care and upkeep of children rather than, for example, the care of the elderly. Grandparents appear as potential childminders and auxiliary carers, particularly in Michael Young and Jean Stogdon's article on the 'vertical' family, which raises, as do others, the question of whether or not grandparents should be paid for the work they perform (for example, if they take the place of foster parents). Most articles are written from the perspective of young to middle-aged educated professional people who wish to have both children and careers, and who are coming up against the obstacles to both. These difficulties have been central to women's lives and choices for the last century, and the positions which are developed here are of particular interest.

Experiential articles by Laura Wilkinson and Jack O'Sullivan speak eloquently of the isolation experienced by the mother of a young baby and the hopes and aspirations to successful parenthood engendered by the first experience of fatherhood. But the recurrent insistence that childcare is a burden for mothers, as if it contained no emotional rewards or intellectual stimulation, is depressing. The vision put forward by Colette Kelleher, Director of the Daycare Trust, of 'children playing with other children in their early excellence centre or after school club, at the bottom of their road or lane - engaging in cultural pursuits, safe and stimulated whilst their parents work', has the distinctly dystopic feel of a layered world of disconnected generations. So too have the various references to 'virtual' childcare through fax, e-mail and other electronic monitoring of teenagers. (As Melanie Howard and Michael Wilmott put it in their discussion of the 'networked family': 'parental monitoring could become progressively more virtual as the child gets older'.)

Those articles which give a flavour of how it is now are more convincing than those which look to an ideal. Liz Bargh challenges the assumption that globalisation will produce greater flexibility by showing that the long hours culture is stronger in the public sector and in big corporations than in small and medium enterprises, where managements are more likely to be responsive to individual needs. She indicates some of the costs the career-friendly parent has to bear, from missing school events to divorce. Fiona McAllister points up a worrying association between child-rearing and the risk of poverty in the mental calculations of the childless. Brad Googins shows that where the corporate model prevails, with 'family friendly' companies hiring the services of child care agencies etc, community services tend to be down-played. Suzan Lewis and Julia Brannen argue that the current strong moral climate of parental responsibility goes along with a slew of policies which are shifting risk from employer to employee and from state to citizen. Peter Moss highlights the current cult of busyness which has gone along with the divisions between time-rich and work-poor families on the one hand and time-poor and work-rich families on the other.

As Googins points out, what the global economy wants is flexible and adaptable *individuals*, a point which brings to mind that other aspect of globalisation: the wandering 'economic' migrants, like the young Chinese found recently dead in a truck at Dover, members of far-flung kinship networks, but isolated from their families. It is a reminder of the diversity of family forms which co-exist now and have done throughout history. It is a notable weakness of the theoretical perspective of many authors here that they posit the existence of one single family form specific to industrialisation - the male breadwinner and female homemaker - and think that one other is emerging to take its place - an egalitarian arrangement based on the working couple. In fact married women have worked in factories in Britain since the industrial revolution, so that the working wife and mother is not a recent product. There has been a diversity of family forms, and of compositions of households, at least since industrialisation. Campaigns around the family are always campaigns *for* one sort of family and *against* others.

It is not until the end of the book that we get a cool look at government policy and its aspiration to forge a new contract with the parent citizen. Maureen Freely emphasises that the word 'parent', although it 'sounds modern and gender-sensitive', is in fact gender-less. She argues that its positive stress on what parents have in common is offset by its obfuscation of the fact that 'mothers and fathers have *different* problems and interests'. It is important to stress this in a book in which, all too often, contributors write as if male and female parents are interchangeable. She also considers the immanent paternalism of the government's approach, with its insistence that parents get it right, as if this was clear-cut. In particular she asks whether a double standard is coming into operation, with interventions directed towards the 'socially excluded' which need not affect the relatively prosperous; she also asks whether consensus is being assumed or imposed rather than discovered through widespread debate (p222). Her concerns echo that expressed by Peter Moss - which arise in general from a reading of *Family Business*: are answers being provided before the critical questions have even been formulated?

Changing Scotland
Jonathan Hearn

Gerry Hassan and Chris Warhurst (eds), *A Different Future: A Modernisers' Guide to Scotland*, Centre for Scottish Public Policy and The Big Issue in Scotland, £10.99

On the back cover of this book the Scottish political journalist Iain MacWhirter describes it as 'the most important book since the seminal *Red Paper on Scotland* edited by Gordon Brown (Edinburgh University Student Publications Board 1975). It is an almost irresistible comparison, echoed more than once between the book's covers. Both volumes attempt comprehensive assessments of Scotland's social, economic and political condition, by rallying impressive teams of contributors from across the fields of academia, public policy, government and community action to comment on diverse aspects of the Scottish situation. However it is a situation that has changed profoundly: *The Red Paper* made an impassioned call in 1975 for the reinvigoration of socialism in the face of economic crisis, growing nationalism, and accelerating demands for devolution; *A Different Future* attempts in 1999 to make sense of the 'new politics' in the 'new Scotland', in the context of a devolved parliament still finding its way in the grey dawn of the twenty-first century. To assess the latter work it is necessary to consider it both in terms of text and context, and to flesh out at points its relationship to its illustrious forerunner.

With thirty-four contributors one can hardly expect *A Different Future* to speak with one voice - it is not a book with a single thesis that can be confronted head on. However, the fact that one of its co-publishers, the Centre for Scottish Public Policy, 'an independent centre left think tank', is closely associated with New Labour in Scotland, not to mention the presence of 'modernisers' in the subtitle, is indicative of the book's general tone. It abounds with programmatic lists of targets that have been or ought to be set, in various areas of governmental reform and policy-making, often foregrounding concern with efficiency and value-for-money, and a deep conviction that we are living in an economy fundamentally transformed by information technologies.

The book is made up of four sections, the first and last grappling more with conceptual frameworks and macro-social institutions and identities, the middle two dealing more directly with economic and social policies. Section One presents various attempts to predict how the new constitutional arrangements will pan out. To the extent that there is a distinctively Scottish political culture or set of social values, perhaps better thought of as a Scottish emphasis on certain tendencies within Britain as a whole, that culture has become entwined with aspirations for, and expectations about self-government. Gerry Hassan argues that complex, multi-layered government will tend to make the SNP's call for independence a moot point. James Mitchell questions the idea of a broad left-of-centre democratic consensus in Scotland, cultivated during the long years of Tory government, suggesting that the new parliament may simply entrench a new, closed, corporatist political elite, remote from popular demands for redistributive economic policies. Lindsay Paterson argues that there *is* a genuine civic sector, distinct from the established managerial elites, that has become mobilised and articulate in its demands, and will not accept a complacent parliament. Tom Nairn reasserts his familiar argument that, although the overdrawn dichotomy between the straight leap to independence and undying unionism was never realistic, Tony Blair's piecemeal project of British constitutional reform is inadequate and ultimately impossible, and will tend to lead towards the long heralded 'break-up of Britain'. George Kerevan (erstwhile Trotskyist and convert from Labour to the SNP) instead heralds the rise of the 'new SNP' peopled by members of the 'Y generation', that is casting off the shackles of social democratic 'tax and spend' ideals for a new high-tech entrepreneurialism. If the SNP of the 1980s and 1990s often sought to out-do 'Old' Labour at its own ideological game, according to Kerevan, anything New Labour can do, the new SNP can do better. Finally, Jack McConnell, Finance Minister for the Scottish Executive, follows suit, suggesting that 'modernisation' is not so much a once and for all transformation of the Labour Party, but an ongoing project, necessitated by a changing and unpredictable future.

Sections Two and Three are more suited to specialist policy tastes, providing impressive coverage in the round. What is most striking here is the oscillation between rather vague but spirited language about the need to realise new standards of economic performance and public provision within an increasingly competitive environment, and tentative suggestions about the structural and macro-level conditions that account for the social and economic problems Scotland faces. Thus, on the one hand, Alf Young's chapter 'Beyond Kvaerner: The Scottish Economy in a Globalising Age' cites American economics guru Stan Davis to argue that Scotland should be making plans on how to out-compete others in the coming 'bio-economy' of genetic engineering, rather than struggling to preserve the remnants of its heavy industries, or becoming complacent about its role in the information economy of computer manufacture. In her chapter on 'Tackling Poverty and Social Exclusion', Scotland's Communities Minister Wendy Alexander relies on the now well-entrenched notion of 'the cycle of intergenerational poverty' (p160) to define the problem, suggesting that access to education and computers are the crux of a solution. On the other hand, in 'Modernising Health: The Paradoxes at the Heart of Policy-Making', Rosie Ilett and Sue Laughlin take pains to show that Scotland's abysmal health record needs to be addressed not simply in terms of the efficiency of the NHS or the sophistication of medical research, but rather in terms of a system of social problems linked to income distribution. And Courtney Peyton and Ian Thomson argue in 'Towards a Sustainable Scotland' that the ultimate economic efficiencies lie in ecologically sensitive and synergistic production systems.

The most salutary contrast with *The Red Paper* is the presence of women's voices and women's concerns, the latter reflected in Esther Breitenbach's chapter on changing gender relations, and Sara Carter and Eleanor Shaw's chapter on 'Bringing Women Into Business'. While the problem of women's social, political, and economic exclusion in Scotland is far from solved, the presence of these concerns in this volume reflects the way the women's movement became integral to the pressures for, and conceptualisation of, the new parliament, including candidate selection procedures that yielded just over 37 per cent women representatives. By contrast there are no MSPs from ethnic minorities, and thus Rowena Arshad's chapter on 'racial inclusion' places a matter too often neglected in Scotland squarely in the main stream of the policy agenda.

The last section looks at 'Governance, Identities and Institutions', examining interrelated adjustments in local government, the public sector, law reform, the civil service, the European Union, and the parliament itself. These chapters are somewhat more informational, summarising how the various structures are being affected by constitutional change. In one of the nicer pieces of writing, Joyce MacMillan questions the idea that Britishness lacks salience in the new Scotland, making a plea for a continuing sense of being British within a complex array of identities, no matter how constitutional arrangements evolve. The book ends with the rather unfocused post-modernesque ruminations of Pat Kane on how Scotland needs to cultivate a 'play ethic' to offset the well worn 'Protestant work ethic' and provide a zone of resistance to burgeoning informational capitalism.

What is the future that this book contemplates 'different' from? Well, it is different from that envisioned in *The Red Paper* of 1975, and understandably so. One could hardly imagine Gordon Brown saying today some of the things he said then in his introduction, to wit: 'Thus, increasingly, the private control of industry has become a hindrance to the further unfolding of the social forces of production'(p14). Such formulas no longer trip off the tongue of the immaculate Chancellor - if they did he would not be in office. And this phrase is only a small expression of the larger marxian socialism thriving at that time, deeply shaped by notions of combined and uneven development, and the potential power of collective action led by the labour movement. *A Different Future* reflects the broadening of leftist thought in the intervening years, to include other kinds of excluded voices, as well as a necessary scepticism about the economic metaphysics of marxism. But while hindsight makes the weaknesses of the old paradigm clearer, it does not totally invalidate it; by comparison, it reminds us of the value of large-scale explanatory frameworks, even if inevitably flawed. For what the newer volume offers is primarily a series of specialised solutions to social problems, without any developed account of the larger structural and interdependent causes of those problems, and a rather uncritical tendency to fall back on notions of the under-cultivation of human potential, rather than an analysis of social forces and distributions of power. The demise of stifling theoretical orthodoxies is not to be regretted, but the absence of vibrant and competing explanatory theories is.

We can read *A Different Future* as it asks us to, as a 'modernisers' guide to Scotland', but we can also read it alongside *The Red Paper*, as a snapshot or artefact of the present historical period. The earlier book reflects the early days of a nationally embedded oppositional politics undergoing consolidation, while the later one speaks of a political generation that has come into its own, been handed somewhat indeterminate levers of power, and is confronted with the immediate problem of learning how to drive this new contraption. These two volumes suggest distinct generational cohorts, Tom Nairn being the only contributor to both volumes. Two of the contributors to the first are now Ministers in the Cabinet at Westminster, while the second boasts four Members of the Scottish Parliament, three of them Ministers in the Executive. But the point of reading *A Different Future* this way is not as an update of who's who in Scottish politics, but rather to remind ourselves, by contrasting the underlying assumptions of two periods in the same place, that the present situation we find ourselves in is itself a product of regnant assumptions in society and politics, which are likely to give way in time, to other ideas and beliefs.

Music and Landscape

Andrew Blake

George McKay, *Glastonbury. A Very English Fair*, Gollancz £14.99
Simon Heffer, *Vaughan Williams* Weidenfeld & Nicolson £12.99

To paraphrase C.L.R. James - what do they know of music who only music know? Despite its physicality (air in motion exciting the eardrums), music seems intangible and mysterious, and it is too often taken for granted as a bringer of pleasure formed within its own symbols. In a world dominated by American popular and European classical genres - which have been made to seem universal thanks to the processes of political and economic control which have ranged from historic imperialism to current globalisation - any writer asking about the ways in which music expresses national characteristics (and who doesn't want to fall back on crude nationalism) has a hard task. In their very different ways, these books attempt to confront the question of a possible musical Englishness. The festival at Glastonbury exists within the world of Anglo-American-global rock, and yet George McKay insists that the festival does indeed embody an identifiable set of national characteristics. Ralph Vaughan Williams studied in London with Victorian composers Stanford and Parry, who believed in a national music but were caught as composers in the German symphonic tradition. He had lessons in Berlin with Max Bruch, and in Paris with Ravel; but, according to Simon Heffer, he remains an unmistakably English musician.

Simon Heffer's brief book - part biography, part essay - is written with warmth and affection. As *Daily Mail* columnist, and author of books on Carlyle and Enoch Powell, as well as the fiercely polemical attempt to construct a post-devolution Englishness (*Nor Shall My Sword*), the reader might expect from Heffer a trenchant, highly personalised view. But such an expectation would be disappointed: Heffer does not construct Vaughan Williams as a right-wing icon. In fact there's surprisingly little social or political argument here: Heffer seems caught by the mystery of music, and is in danger of failing the James test. Yet he does not deny Vaughan Williams's socialist leanings, and he documents the composer's refusal to accept official titles (or any honour other than the Order of Merit) alongside the generosity of the Vaughan Williams Trust, which has funded innumerable performances of work by younger composers. There is no overt Euroscepticism here, either: the composer's attitude to modernism, and contemporary European music in general, is mentioned in passing, rather than forming the centre of the argument.

... which is, very simply, that Vaughan Williams was a great English composer. He was one of a number of musicians trying, in the Edwardian years, to establish a national musical language. Cecil Sharp was collecting folk song, and so did Vaughan Williams, who said that it freed him from foreign influence. Elgar was writing choral and orchestral music which was not *quite* Germanic (the cantata *Caractacus*, for example), and so did Vaughan Williams: *Toward the Unknown Region*, the *Sea Symphony*, and *Five Mystical Songs* all combine an Elgar-like feel for the oratorio tradition's massed choirs with interests in metaphysical poetry, the poems of Walt Whitman, and the modal church music of the Tudor era. Despite his agnosticism, Vaughan Williams recognised the importance of religious music for his national project; he edited several collections of hymns and carols, and in the *Fantasia on a Theme of Thomas Tallis* (1910), he made possible the use of those modes for large-scale contemporary composition. His own compositional style, while it later acknowledged jazz, big band dance music and the sonic tendencies of European modernism, was rooted in this moment.

So Vaughan Williams had become musically English by the outbreak of the first world war. Thereafter he became increasingly culturally English. His music reflects, and is involved in, the upheavals and changes of the inter-war years, portraying an anxious, almost pacifist, foreboding. The pastoral mode, while not extinguished, becomes paralleled by the harsher and more dissonant language employed in the fourth symphony and piano concerto, whose final and strongest echo is in the post-1945 war symphony, the sixth. But during this time Vaughan Williams was involved in the formation of cultural policy (broadcasting and lecturing on national music), and with what could be called musical communalism, writing music for amateur performance and for film, including official war films. And, most importantly in this regard, he was involved in the planning and musical provision for festivals, notably the Leith Hill festival based at Dorking, in the Surrey hills, where he lived from the age of two (in 1874) until his death in 1958. The festival of necessity involves music's relation with a particular place and landscape (and, often disruptively, with the local temporal and social order), and Vaughan Williams's contribution to the English musical festival was an important aspect of his contribution to musical Englishness as a whole.

W hile Vaughan Williams was collecting folk song in an attempt to escape from the overwhelming musicality of Richard Wagner, the composer Rutland Boughton had been emulating Wagner's achievement in composing long operas based on national legend, and then setting up a festival dedicated to the performance of this work in a small provincial town (Bayreuth in Wagner's case). Boughton wrote a sequence of operas based on Tennyson's Arthurian poetry cycle *The Idylls of the King,* and then set up his festival, in Glastonbury in Somerset. The first performance was held in the Assembly Rooms on 5 August 1914, the day after the outbreak of the first world war; after a break during the rest of the 1914-8 conflict (in which Boughton served, as did Vaughan Williams), the festival was repeated until 1926.

There's no *direct* connection between these events and the Glastonbury Festival which takes place at the farm of Michael Eavis (Worthy Farm, Pilton, a few miles from Glastonbury). George McKay doesn't try to make one, and, wisely, he doesn't even make the Boughton festivals his starting point; instead, he turns to the country house jazz festivals of the late 1950s, and the founding of the Notting Hill carnival, as the precursors of the outdoor rock festival. In a thematically arranged sequence of essays, we are led back to that first Glastonbury festival through McKay's personal evocations of the 1999 festival, and his explorations of festival culture and its politics in the recent past, which is followed by a central chronology of festivals in Britain since the 1950s. McKay also explores aspects of Glastonbury's relationship with the area's mystical traditions and its landscapes, and the politics of the environment and the peace movements which have been the ostensible beneficiaries of Eavis's events.

The reader will also approach George McKay with foreknowledge; in this case the expectation is more clearly fulfilled. The author of *Senseless Acts of Beauty, Cultures of Resistance Since the Sixties,* and editor of *DIY Culture: Party and Protest in Nineties Britain,* sees the festival movement in Britain, and Glastonbury in particular, as an aspect of the troubled politics of leisure and lifestyle - this has involved successive waves of demonised youth cultures and their hedonistic pursuits on the one hand, and an anxious and repressive state on the other. Tracing the political opposition to festivals, the various parliamentary enquiries and laws such as the 1994 Criminal Justice Act, and discussing the ways in which those criminalised by such laws have responded, McKay is able to set up the Glastonbury festival as a particular kind of liminal, carnival event, in which the worlds of the various alternative cultures and those of mainstream society, with its policing of property and of propriety, come into juxtaposition. Some festivals - such as the Caslemorton rave of 1992 - are merely internal to the group, reinforcing its own solidarity (and puzzling or angering outsiders). Eavis's Glastonbury festival, on the other hand, which is licensed, policed, and attended by significant numbers of different ages and classes (if not, to this observer, ethnicities), acts as a borderline, which people can blur or cross, and/or over which they can see each other more clearly than at other times.

In this way the festival acts as a portal, a gate between worlds; and this is a role, as George McKay demonstrates, that has been imposed on Glastonbury at least since the legend of Joseph of Arimethea's landing in Britain was first propagated (Joseph brought the Holy Grail and planted the Glastonbury Thorn). Since the time that the Christian legend took hold, twisting itself around the equally powerful legends of King Arthur, a cluster of pilgrims, novelists, poets, seers and mystics have found their inspiration here; and since the Glastonbury settlement is far older than Christianity, a pre-Arthurian pagan tendency, expressed in the legends of the Isle of Avalon, is also reflected in the events of the festival. The pyramidal design of the main stage, the hedonism of the sometimes alternative-cultural festival-goers, and the bands who play at the festivals; all are aspects of a general Glastonbury mysticism which accompanies the music. This mysticism was present in the 1960s, as in the 1920s; but in the early twenty-first century it has become common. It's hard to see the current pervasiveness of a kind of weak New-Ageism as 'alternative'; and if, in the current Buffy- and Harry Potter-worshipping climate, a more general Manichean paganism has pervaded the cultural mainstream, so much the more difficult for those who wish to present themselves as the holders of an authentic national or local culture, or as opponents of this multi-tributaried mainstream.

George McKay records and juxtaposes these tendencies with an agnosticism worthy of Vaughan Williams. He reads the spiritual tomes and accounts of ley lines, and interviews musicians, festival-goers, organisers and the police, with an informed scepticism, registering the various accounts of utopia or dystopia with a dry eye. His chief concern, as with *Senseless Acts*, is to re-inscribe these events as part of a cultural history, and in particular a cultural history of active popular opposition. So while he disconnects the Glastonbury festivals of the 1920s from the Pilton festivals of the 1990s, he also reconnects them, finding counter-cultural people who have used the Assembly Rooms in recent times for musical and social purposes; when he talks of festivals in history, he takes us back to the medieval fairs of East Anglia, with their carnivalesque upturning of the status quo.

George McKay passes the C.L.R. James test with flying colours. Only when he has outlined the political, mystical and historical lineages of the Glastonbury festival does he turn to its music, and then in outline rather than detail. There is no list of greatest-ever sets, or vintage years; little sense of what it is like to perform for the seething mass in front of the main stage. He identifies the changing tendencies among genres, noting with approval that more space is now made for dance music. Englishness here - and he continually implies that Englishness is at the heart of the festival - is more about making a space for music to be heard, and experienced positively in the right political and social context, than it is about sound itself.

And that, surely, is the point - of both these books (a liberal, with cultural-relativist tendencies, writes). There is no single tradition of English music or music-making; there are dozens of lineages and derivations, including classical composition, the various mutations of rock music, and DJ-led genres such as techno and drum'n'bass. Lacking fierce associations of musical form with national or ethnic identity, or with the purely commercial - which have characterised much musical experience elsewhere - music in twentieth century Britain was more polymorphous and internationalist, related to but never dominated by classes and subcultures. The festivals, connecting the local with the global and the landscape with sound, have been crucial to making our experience of music in culture quite literally grounded (rather than abstract, mysterious and aerial), and for that we may thank among many others Ralph Vaughan Williams and Michael Eavis. They, and we, know more of music than mere sound.

After success – the politics of civil society

After success - the politics of civil society

Andreas Hess

In 1989, the year of the two-hundredth anniversary of the French Revolution, Europe presented itself with the best possible celebratory gift: the fall of the Berlin Wall became a symbol not just for the collapse of communist regimes, but for all that has come to be regarded as the positive side of the bequest of the French Revolution - the discovery of civil society, of 'society acting for and by itself' (Tocqueville), human rights, freedom.

However, the record is not as positive - or as simple - as it seems at first sight. As Francois Furet, a famous scholar of the French Revolution, reminded us, the achievements of 1989 were by no means self-evident. Indeed the supporters and sympathisers of the Russian Revolution of 1917 had themselves always regarded the French Revolution as a model - and as 'unfinished business'. Thus, the Russian revolutionaries desperately tried to correct what they considered the 'negative outcomes' of 'La Grande Révolution': the difference between bourgeois and citizen, and between equal political rights and substantive social inequality. In the end - and in the logic of their struggle to literally 'draw even' - the Russian revolutionaries got rid of all the vital arteries of a 'go-between' public sphere; they abolished any sphere in which contradictions and ideas could be acted on and tested out freely. As a consequence, the coercive state replaced civil society - until the cunning reason of history took its revenge in 1989.

Thus the corrective attempt of the Russian Revolution and other Soviet-led systems failed, at least partly because of these built-in problems. Marxism, with its critique of the contradictions of civil society, advanced the idea of overall and absolute equality as an outcome of class struggle - thereby forgetting that a completely conflict-free society would also mean the end of any genuinely meaningful concept of 'the political'. In this logic of class struggle, and with the increasing - if not to say inflationary - importance of 'the social', 'the political' becomes merely a derivative. This, together with the abolition of a functioning public sphere, led to a situation in the former socialist countries where the private did indeed become political, and where an unpublished poem, read out in private, could lead to deportation and physical elimination (as happened in the case of Osip Mandelstam).

A case could be made for the historical acquittal of Marxism, by arguing that Stalin had no knowledge of Marx, or that he was never a real Marxist. But that would be to give Marxism an almost theology-like status, in that the true moment of revelation never comes. As the critical theorist Adorno once pointed out, the course taken by civilisation, from its early beginnings to the barbarism experienced in the twentieth century, could not have been conceived of *in advance*; however, as he also pointed out, with hindsight and *retrospectively* things always look different. If Adorno's remark is correct, then it might be appropriate to say that it was not inevitable that Marx's theory led to the politics of Soviet-style regimes and Stalinism; in hindsight, however, it is not too difficult to see the holes in Marxism that helped to contribute to its dogmatisation, and to the creation of 'actually existing communism'. It was a project which denounced human rights and the rule of law as bourgeois, a project for which the instrumental and tactical treatment of 'the political' was paramount - in other words, a project that was extremely relativist when it came to values - and one should thus always have been prepared for the worst.

In Britain, however, the worst case scenarios of totalitarianism - whether national socialist or fascist or Stalinist - have never developed. Obviously, the fact that Britain has never experienced any of these regimes, or any of the upheavals that so many other European societies have been through, is regarded as a good thing. Britain has usually been a bystander, under threat and occasionally hurt by events in continental Europe, but never invaded or occupied. However, the dialectical, twisted, outcome of this is that, not having suffered any of these extreme experiences, Britain has become complacent. It has never had to radically review its political arrangements and institutions. While continental Europe has experienced ruptures, in Britain a sense of continuity has prevailed; and this has helped to form a political culture that speaks of radical events but has never experienced them - and this brings us back to the events of 1989.

Everywhere in Europe '1989' left major fault-lines. Apart from a few Marxist sects (whose business is naturally to believe), the left in continental Europe tried to take on the lessons of 1989. It is probably fair to say that no-one today promotes a model of social justice in which personal freedom doesn't figure prominently. In particular, the concept of civil society, and the prominent role that the public sphere plays in it, has undergone a renaissance. To be sure, we are talking about a different concept of civil society. There has not been a return to what Jeffrey Alexander has called 'civil society 1': civil society as conceptualised by Adam Ferguson, Hegel and other enlightenment thinkers, as including all activities and institutions which were not directly linked to the state. Nor are we talking of 'civil society 2', the version criticised by Marx as being determined only by capitalist interest. Rather we are talking of 'civil society 3', which corresponds to a society that has become differentiated, one in which the binary opposition of state and civil society has been enriched by various 'in-between' institutions, mainly in the public sphere. It is this latter concept of civil society which is now being used, as a normative as well as descriptive starting point.

The civil society concept is now used as a normative concept of democracy: it provides the means to criticise 'actually existing democracy'; it thus serves the purpose of making democracy more democratic. As Alexander has pointed out:

> Civil society ... should not be equated with trust in an actual government, although it is a necessary condition for that. To trust faithfully in the good of any actual government, indeed, would be abandon universalism for the particularism of a party or state. Civil society ... means trust in the universalistic values that abstract from any particular society and that provide critical leverage against particular historical actors. It guarantees the

existence of the public, not public consensus or consent. Because of their trust in a higher universal order, citizens continually make demands for authorities to justify their actions. The higher order embodies ideal justice; because earthly authorities must inevitably violate this ideal norm, moral outrage is a continual result. In strong civil societies, then, distrust or authoritative action and political conflict are omnipresent. Yet it is the very separation from the endorsement of particular arrangements that makes democracy possible.[1]

However, none of these insights are deployed in the political discussions of the liberal left in the United Kingdom today. More than ten years after the fall of the Berlin Wall, Charter 88 is still fighting for institutional arrangements that have been practised in Western Continental Europe and the United States for decades, and for one decade now in Eastern Europe. The rest of the left in Britain is fighting the good fight but has got lost in a Gramscian war of cultural trenches, in which it is more important to be politically correct than to radically change the institutions. (As it turns out, however, the institutional logic almost always prevails, and is harder to subvert than is generally assumed.) Ironically, the society that invented the very concept of civil society no longer fights for its potential achievements. In the United Kingdom the key ingredients for a blossoming civil society, namely republican discourse, and a rhetoric of virtue and rights, appear to be completely marginalised.

In such a situation it is always helpful to take a closer look around. The special theme of this issue of *Soundings* presents some 'snapshots' of the contemporary international debate on civil society 'after its success'. This collection doesn't aim at completeness, nor does it follow one set view; rather it aims to make pluralistic views known. The essays represent an attempt to circumnavigate the notion of complex civil society, and to make some inroads into the field - they do not aim to give the definitive account of the notion (that would be something that would go against the grain of the whole concept of civil society). This theme section of *Soundings* is representative of work in

---

1. Jeffrey Alexander, 'Some Notes on the Misunderstanding of Civil Society as Capitalism', presented at 'The Direction of Contemporary Capitalism Conference', University of Sussex, April 1996.

the field, and introduces approaches which amount to what could be called a 'critical pro-civil society position': a position which contrasts a normative, almost 'ideal-type', concept of civil society with the empirical environment, the 'real world' of civil society. The aim is to find new, non-dogmatic, ways of thinking about contemporary society. Particularly for the liberal left in this country, it is important in this debate not to follow the paths of already existing political camps, and/or well-worn ways of thinking - i.e. to avoid conceptualising society either in old-fashioned Marxist terms, or through super-modern, yet no-substance Third Way soundbites. In short, the aim is to think imaginatively about contemporary society and not to fall into the traps that have previously beguiled hyper-critical Marxist approaches, Gramscian culturalists, dogmatic critical theorists (yes, they do exist) and Third Way apologists.

In the first essay Jeffrey C. Alexander makes a fresh attempt to theorise civil society, by looking at its uncivil dimensions. He suggests that it is crucial to think about contemporary civil society through making distinctions, to see for example that uncivil particularisms when developed into the extreme can challenge the existing order. Those particularisms are thus in conflict with concepts and understandings of civil society whose very nature it is to strive for universal values. In this respect Alexander re-conceptualises an old sociological problem, namely that of how much conflict can be allowed (or is even necessary) while at the same time achieving societal consensus and preventing society from drifting apart.

Robert Fine, in his critique of John Keane, one of the chief promoters of the concept of civil society, looks at such 'uncivil' extremes as violence and terror, events that challenge the idea of 'neat' civil society. Fine criticises Keane's work for not reflecting appropriately the intrinsic relationship that exists between civil society and violence. Linked to the question of violence is the problem of radical evil. Maria Pia Lara asks how discourses that deal with the uncivil dimensions of civil society can be represented, and can have an impact on societies' collective learning process, without destroying the public sphere, the crucial backbone of civil society. With reference to Walter Benjamin and Hannah Arendt, she suggests that it is narratives in particular, and the way evil is narrated in the public sphere, that can be empowering in this respect. William Outhwaite approaches the idea of civil society from a very different angle. In contrast to the Eurosceptics, he suggests that a European perspective could serve as a new starting point for reflection. However, reflecting about a common European civil society is not the same thing as discussing civil societies *in* Europe. Claire Wallace investigates the real problems of encounters when 'Europe meets Europe'. In her contribution she reflects on her own experience - the major contradictions and culture clashes that can arise when western feminist values meet the post-1989 world of Eastern Europe. Finally, Jonathan Freedland comments upon the problems faced by prospective citizens - and the cause of republican renewal - in the United Kingdom these days. This contribution can be read as a further comment on William Outhwaite's 'federal' European perspective.

Grazyna Kubica-Heller is a social anthropologist, writer and photographer living in Poland. It seems appropriate to supplement our special feature on the civil society debate with her photographs of people from East Central Europe, who have waited such a long time for the idea of civil society to prevail.

Four of the papers published here (by Alexander, Fine, Pia Lara and Outhwaite) were first presented at the symposium 'The Uncivil Dimensions of Civil Society', which took place in Gregynog, Wales in September 1999. We would like to thank the University of Wales Research Fund and the School of Social Sciences at the University of Wales, Bangor for supporting and contributing to the organisation of the symposium. Unfortunately not all of the excellent papers presented at the conference could be published in the journal. However, the symposium was very much a collective effort, and thanks must go to all contributors. We would also like to thank the Vienna-based journal Transit *in which Claire Wallace's article first appeared in German in an edited form (*Transit *Number 9, 1995).*

Contradictions

The uncivilising pressures of space, time and function

Jeffrey C. Alexander

In the civil society debate Jeffrey C. Alexander stands out as a key contributor. In this essay he points towards a critical revision of the very idea of civil society and our understanding of it.

My goal in this discussion is to give flesh and blood to the concept of 'civil society' - the skeleton concept that has hung in the closet of social theory for centuries, but has never been considered in a sufficiently empirical way. Theories of modernisation, development and rationalisation have assumed that broader solidary structures are created in the course of social development, as offshoots of other, more visible and more familiar structural processes - such as urbanisation, marketisation, socialisation, bureaucratisation, and secularisation. I would argue, on the contrary, that the construction of a wider and more inclusive sphere of solidarity must be studied in itself. From the beginning of its appearance in human societies, civil society has been organised, insofar as it has been organised at all, around its own particular cultural codes. It has been able to broadcast its idealised image of social relationships because it has been organised by certain kinds of communicative institutions; and departures from these relationships have been sanctioned or rewarded in more material terms by certain kinds of regulative institutions. Civil society has been sustained, as well, by distinctive kinds of personality structures and by forms of interaction that are of an unusual kind.

In thinking about such an 'independent' sphere of civil solidarity, the social theorist must walk along a delicate line. The codes, institutions and interactions that compose such a sphere must be considered in themselves, as structures in their own right. Their status cannot simply be read off from the condition of the spheres which surround civil society; they are not simply dependent variables. At the same time, the very briefest consideration makes it clear that, in a concrete sense, these internal modes of organisation are always deeply interpenetrated with the rest of society. At every point they are connected to activities in other spheres. They reach out beyond civil society narrowly conceived to set standards and create images in other spheres. Conversely, what happens in other spheres of society - what is possible and what not - has fundamental effects on the structure and operation of culture, institutions and interactions in civil society.

Indeed, the tension between what might be called the internal and external references of civil society is not merely a theoretical issue; it is a central empirical and ideological concern. To the degree that civil society gains autonomy from other spheres, to that degree it can define social relationships in a more consistently universalistic way. The binary structure of the discourse of civil society suggests that, even in the most ideal circumstances, this universalism will never be achieved in anything more than a highly proximate way. Because social reality is far from ideal, moreover, the autonomy of civil society normally is continually compromised and reduced. The exigencies of non-civil spheres, institutions and modes of interaction permeate civil society, and the discourse of repression is applied far and wide. The world of the 'we' becomes narrowed; the world of the 'they' becomes larger and assumes multifarious forms. It is not only groups outside of the nation state that are disqualified from gaining entrance to civil society, but many groups inside it as well.

It is to a systematic model of these boundary processes that I will devote this essay. In this task, 'idealist', or rather idealising, approaches to civility and the public sphere will not be of much help. Whether critical or apologetic, such approaches have suggested that civil society should be able to stand on its own and eliminate the influence of these other spheres: otherwise it will not be able to stand at all. From Aristotle and Rousseau to Arendt and Habermas, idealistic thinkers have embraced the utopianism of civil society, not as a regulating idea, or norm, but as a possible expression of real society. They have argued that it is possible to create a social system that is thoroughly civil, solidaristic, altruistic, and inclusive, a social system that is homologous with civil society itself. They have dismissed the economic world as the world of 'necessity', one from which normative ideas of reciprocity are excluded *tout court*. They have rejected the political world as inherently bureaucratic and instrumental, as resting always and everywhere on domination alone. These 'systems' are conceived as inherently uncivil, as colonisers of the lifeworld of a solidary sphere that is doomed because it is vulnerable, by definition, to spheres of a stronger, more material kind. In a similar way, religion is conceived as an inherently dominating sphere, for it grounds understanding in a closed manner that is opposed to the open-ended and universalistic dialogue that marks civil understanding.

These approaches are not wrong in that they make forceful criticisms of the non-civil sphere. Indeed, I will make generous use of these and other such criticisms in my discussion below. These approaches err, rather, because they ignore the necessity for functional differentiation and complexity, not only in an institutional sense but in a moral one. The more developed the society, the more there emerge different kinds of institutional spheres and discourses. To be sure, the realisation of civil society is restricted by these spheres; at the same time, however, the civil sphere enters into institutional and moral interchanges with these worlds, despite the fact that they are of a very different kind. This interpenetration can cut both ways: civil society can colonise these other spheres; it is not simply a case of being colonised by them. To avoid the idealist fallacy, we must recognise that civil society is always nested in the practical worlds of the uncivil spheres, and we must study the compromises and fragmentations, the 'real' rather than merely idealised civil society, that results.

Civil society is instantiated in the real because social systems exist in real space, because they have been constructed in real time, and because they must perform functions that go beyond the construction of solidarity itself. Instantiation reduces the ideal of equal and free participation - it compromises and fragments the potentially civil sphere - by attaching status to primordial qualities that have nothing to do with one's status in civil society as such. Primordial qualities are those attributed to persons by virtue of their membership in a particular group, one that is thought to be based on unique qualities which those outside the group can, by definition, never hope to attain. Such qualities can be analogised to physical attributes like race and blood; but

(see page 102/3) *the idea that something always been around / in existence from beginning when in 'fact' may not have been.*

almost any social attribute can assume a primordial position. Language, race, national origins, religion, class, intelligence and region - all these have been primordialised at different historical conjunctures. In different times and in different places, actors have become convinced that only those possessing certain versions of these qualities have what it takes to become members of civil society. They have believed that individuals and groups who do not possess these qualities must be uncivilised and cannot be included. 'Civil' in this way becomes contrasted with 'primordial'. The truth, of course, is that the very introduction of particular criteria is uncivil. Civil primordiality is a contradiction in terms.

Space: the geography of civil society

Civil society is idealised, by philosophers and by lay members alike, as a universalistic and abstract 'space', an open world without limits, an endless horizon. In fact, however, territory is basic to any real existing historical society. Territory converts the space of civil society into a particular 'place'. Civil society can become unique and meaningful, in fact, only as a particular place. It is not just some place, or any place, but our place, a 'centre', a place that is different from places that are outside its territory. Attachment to this central place becomes primordialised. As it becomes a primordial quality, territory divides; it becomes articulated with the binary discourse of civil society. The capacity for liberty becomes limited to those who have their feet on the sacred land, and the institutions and interaction of civil society become distorted and segmented in turn.

Nationalism can be conceived, in this sense, as the pollution of space that is demarcated by the territorial limits of states. Civility had, of course, always been circumscribed by centres, but before the sixteenth century these primordial territories had been conceived more locally, as villages, cities, regions, or simply as the physical areas inhabited by extended kinship networks and tribes. Beginning in the Renaissance, however, territory began to be viewed nationally. Attachment to one's place meant connection to the land of the nation. It is important to see that this geographical bifurcation was held to be true no matter how the national territory was defined, whether it was defined as a national community of language and blood, as in the German case, or an abstract universal community of ideas, as in post-revolutionary France. No matter how it was defined, only members of this nation were seen as capable of reason, honesty, openness, and civility; members of others nations were not. Membership in other national territories seemed to generate dishonesty, distrust, and secrecy. They were naturally enemies.

This extraordinary restriction on universalism has had extraordinary consequences for the real history of civil societies. One consequence has been the continuous intertwining of real civil societies and war, the ultimate expression of relationships of an uncivil kind. Kant believed that democracies would never make war on other democracies; he suggested that the qualities of universalism and reason that characterised such societies would incline them to dialogue rather than force and would make it difficult for them to stereotype and brutalise people on the other side. But the democratic quality of other nations is always something that is very much open to debate, and the territorial bifurcation of civil charisma makes the civility of others much more difficult to discern. This explains why, throughout the history of civil societies, war has been a sacred obligation; to wage war against members of other territories has been simultaneously a national and a civilising task. Ancient Athens, the first real if limited democracy, whose polis has formed the model for civil societies until today, waged continuous war against its neighbouring city states, fighting against the barbarism that foreign territory implied. For the Renaissance city states in Italy, military glory was a central virtue, and their publics defended and extended their civil societies by waging war against 'foreign', yet equally civil communities in their national clime. The imperial expansion of Northern European nations from the sixteenth through to the nineteenth centuries certainly had economic motives; but it was inspired, as well, by the urgent need to civilise those who were enemies of civilisation because they were not fortunate enough to be nurtured in the same part of the earth as they.

But it is the great 'imperial republics', as Raymond Aron called them, that demonstrate this territorial bifurcation of civility in the most striking way. When the English and French fought against each other from the sixteenth through to the nineteenth centuries, they were societies that resembled each other in fundamental ways, each considering itself to possess a fundamentally civil, if not democratic dimension of social life. Yet elites and common people alike were in each nation convinced that it was only their national territories that allowed them to breathe free. Were the motives of Napoleonic France any different in their wars of forced national liberation, which placed in the same polluted categories the 'enslaved' citizens of nations as diverse as Egypt and Germany, not to mention Italy and, potentially, England itself? And then there is the centuries-long military history of the very democratic United States, whose every war has been fought as a ritual sacrifice so that the oppressed of other countries may be Americanised, and free. This is not to say that many of these wars have not, in fact, been exercises in self-defence or national liberation. It is to suggest, however, that the connection between national territory and the binary discourse of civil societies has been striking indeed, and that it has always and everywhere inspired wars of an atrocious and punitive kind.

'membership in other national territories seems to generate dishonesty, distrust and secrecy'

The nationalist understanding of civility, moreover, has had fragmenting consequences of an internal kind. It has allowed those who have been excluded from civil society to be constructed as 'foreigners' and aligned with the territorial enemies of the nation against which wars are waged. Those who are excluded are often seen, in other words, not only as uncivil but as genuine threats to national security. In America, this has taken the form of 'nativism', defined by John Higham as the 'intense opposition to an internal minority on the grounds of its foreign connection'. In the course of American history, indeed, virtually every immigrant group has been subject to this construction, from Indians to African-Americans, from Catholic immigrants to Jews, from Germans in World War I to Japanese in World War II. There is no need to multiply examples of this kind, or to explain how French anti-semitism turned Dreyfus into a German spy, and German Nazism turned the Jewish 'nation' into the emblem of international capitalist conspiracy which was threatening the independence of the German state. Such facts are well known, but their theoretical implications are not well understood. The problem is not just that extremists and fundamentalists have so often threatened the tranquillity of democratic life. It is an issue of a much more systemic kind.

Because civil society is territorial and spatially fixed, it produces its own enemies. Even in the most civil of societies the discourse of liberty is bifurcated in a territorial manner. In making pollution primordial, this bifurcation makes repression more likely. This is why, in their quest for inclusion into the world of civil society, the excluded so often try to re-represent themselves as patriots. During the rise of German anti-semitism in Weimar, Jewish organisations widely publicised the fact that tens of thousands of their compatriots had died for the Kaiser. Throughout their long struggle for inclusion, champions of the African-American community have pointed proudly to the fact that blacks have fought willingly in every major American war, beginning with the Revolution itself. According to T. H. Marshall, it was the patriotic participation of the British working class in World War II that created the cross-class solidarity that formed the basis for the postwar creation of the welfare state.

If nationalism restricts civility by bifurcating space 'outside' the nation, regionalism recreates a similar if sometimes less violent restriction for space within the nation. It is not only nations that are centres, but also, very conspicuously, the cities and regions within them. These domestic centres primordialise the discourse of liberty, constructing the periphery as lacking the charisma of national civility, as a kind of foreign territory inside the nation itself. City and country was for centuries one of the most pernicious distinctions of this kind. The German burgher proverb, 'the city air makes us free', was intended to be much more than a sociological observation about the effects of legal rights. Throughout the history of European civil societies peasants were likened to animals or, in the inimitable phrase of Karl Marx, to 'lumps of clay'. Regional divisions like North and South, and East and West, have always and everywhere carried a surplus of meaning. These regional divisions have fragmented the civil society of nations, its culture, its interactions, and often its regulative and communicative institutions. When they have overlapped with other kinds of exclusions - economic, ethnic, political, or religious - they have formed the basis for repressive closure movements, for the construction of ghettos, for brutal and aggressive exercises in forced incorporation, and for secessionist movements and for civil wars.

Time: civil society as historical sedimentation

Just as civil societies are always created in real space, so they are always created in real time. The utopian idea of civility suggests a timeless realm where people have always been thus, and always will be. Yet every civil society has actually been started, by somebody, at a particular time; and in virtually every territorial space different regimes of more and less civil societies have been started over and over again.

What is important about this temporality is that it becomes primordialised.

The time of origin of virtually every community is treated as a sacred time, one that is mythologised in national narratives and replicated by periodic rituals of remembrance. The founders of this community are sacralised as well. A charisma of time attaches to the founders of civil societies, who were there 'at the beginning'. Myths of origins not only give to these founders pride of place, but they attribute their accomplishment to the primordial characteristics of this founding group: to their religion, their race, their class, their language, to their country of origins if it is different from the nation they founded at a later time. The origin myths of civil society narrate the founders' role in terms of the discourse of liberty, but the capacity for liberty is temporalised. Only the primordial characteristics of the founding group, it is widely believed, allowed them to succeed in founding the national society at a such a propitious historical time.

I f the characteristics of the founders are equated with the pure categories of civil society, it is only logical in a cultural sense that the qualities of those who come after them, insofar as they differ from the founders' own, should in turn be equated with the impure categories of this civil discourse. Temporality, in other words, creates a time order of civility, a rank order of categorical qualities that become the basis for claims of privilege within civil society itself. In American history, each new immigrant group has been considered polluted in certain crucial respects. The inability to speak English properly has been attributed to an incapacity for rationality and clarity. The extended kinship networks that typify the early forms of ethnic communities have been seen as a manifestation of closed rather than open behaviour, as breeding factionalism rather than open competition, as manifestations of secrecy rather than openness and trust. Different religious practices are invariably considered to be inferior ones, characterised in terms of emotionality rather than control and hierarchy rather than equality. The result is not simply 'discrimination' but repulsion and fear. There is the suspicion that these later arriving groups are outside the very categories of civil society itself. Can the newly arrived Irish immigrants ever, in fact, become good Americans? Can Jews? Can the newly arrived immigrants from China and Japan? How is it possible, since they are so different from us?

Yet, if peremptory arrival creates such bifurcations, the passing of time can also blur them. Ethnic succession is not simply an economic fact, created by ecological and material pressures that allow one group to leave a niche and

[handwritten margin notes: outsiders seen an. uncivil founder seen as civil.]

another to enter it. It is a cultural learning process that may be tempered by time. Familiarity does not lead to understanding exactly; rather, it leads to identification, a process that interpolates both space and time. Long term presence in the primordial place often cleanses and purifies primordial qualities, allowing what were once considered fundamentally different characteristics to be seen, instead, as variations on a common theme. This is not an evolutionary process that happens automatically. Bridging, connecting, and transversing is a project, one carried out by temporally disprivileged groups themselves. Making use of the communicative and the regulatory institutions of civil society, they demand to be reconsidered in more civil terms. In 'ethnic' literature, for example, writers re-represent their group's primordial qualities in terms of the 'common tradition', in both an aesthetic and a moral sense. They offer alternative framings of primordial traits, using humour, tragedy, or romance to allay danger and create a sense of familiarity. Immigrant social movements and well-known immigrant personalities present themselves as embodying traditional civil qualities. They argue that they are revivifying the national discourse of liberty, and that their ethnic qualities are complementary analogues of the very characteristics exhibited by the founding groups.

To understand fully the implications of temporality, however, one must see that the origins of a civil community are also reconstructed in a manner that is much less voluntaristic than the pacific qualities of immigration imply. The temporal concreteness of civil societies means that their foundings interrupted and displaced societies at some earlier time. They may have emerged from revolutionary upheavals against a more conservative or more radical regime; they may have been founded upon the military conquest of native peoples or resident national groups; they may have involved domination via purchase through commercial treaties or through political acquisition of a less direct type. When the radical English parliament organised its political revolution against kingship, it did not merely emphasise the expansion of civil society; rather, it presented its revolution as a victory of a different 'ethnic' group, the Anglo-Saxons, over the Royalist blood line. The French revolutionaries did not only make a universal and democratic insurrection, but they proclaimed a victory for the Gauls over the Francs. The American Revolution also involved temporal displacement, not only victory over the native American aboriginal peoples but over ethnic peoples who were not Anglo-Saxon in type. Whatever the specific manner of displacement, the primordial characteristics of the dominated group are stigmatised; they are represented in terms of impure categories of the triumphant civil state. Civil society is, at its very origins, fragmented and distorted in what are often the most heinous ways.

These distorted self-understandings of civil society set off chain reactions that often invite 'refoundings' of an equally violent type. The repercussions of such posterior reconstructions can produce physical displacement and ghettoisation. Apartheid in South Africa occurred after the Afrikaaner 'refounding' of the earlier settler society founded by the English. When the Nazis refounded Germany as an Aryan and Christian state, it produced not merely physical displacement and coercion but mass extermination. Refoundings can produce centuries of struggles for liberation and oppression, which often lead to civil war, as did America's racial caste system, which was intrinsic to the founding of a civil society of the most profoundly democratic type.

The temporal bifurcations of civil societies, it is clear, intertwine with fragmentations founded on territory, particularly because both involve constructions that refer to the foundings of national societies. The primordial qualities that societies identify with liberty refer to founders who were 'there at the beginning'. When excluded national groups re-represent themselves as patriots, as people whose contributions to national security have been unfairly ignored, they are not only symbolically inserting themselves into the particular place of the nation but also into its historical time. Because historical memory preserves the charisma of time, it is always disputed by groups who are temporally displaced. Originating events, and later critical historical ones as well, are continually reconstituted in order to legitimate a new primordial definition of civility. Groups who have been excluded or dominated reconstrue their nation's history so that civility is described in broader and more expansive ways; groups which are threatened try to maintain more restrictive primordial definitions, or even to make them more narrow still. Social movements use communicative institutions to convince the public that 'history' must be revised; they use regulatory institutions to force the public to make illegal the laws that are implied by this outmoded version of history. (Note here the open conflict over the Statue of Liberty between new ethnic groups and the old Plymouth Rock Americans in the early 1900s.)

Function: the destruction of boundary relations and their repair

Societies are more than 'collectivities' framed by time and rooted in space. They are enormously complex social systems whose institutions become increasingly specialised, separated from one another not only by the differentiation of their physical organisation and staff, but also by the normative understandings that inform and regulate them. The possibility of institutional and cultural differentiation into increasingly separate spheres lies, of course, at the very heart of the notion of civil society that I have been advancing here. Its capacity for justice, for equality and liberty, its very existence, depends upon the creation of a space that can stand outside spheres of a more restrictive kind. Yet, as I have suggested in one way or another throughout this essay, this autonomy must be understood in a dialectical way. The very independence that makes civil society possible also makes it vulnerable.

There is a dangerous and fundamentally illusory tendency in classical and modern social theory: to understand functional differentiation as a process that contributes to stability and individuation. Functional differentiation may be integrative and ennobling, but it is by no means necessarily so. If the solidarity and universalism of civil society form one dimension of the social system, these qualities are challenged by spheres abutting civil society which have radically different functional concerns - which operate according to contradictory goals, employ different kinds of media, and produce social relations of an altogether different sort. The goal of the economic sphere is wealth, not justice in the civil sense; it is organised around efficiency, not solidarity, and depends upon hierarchy, not equality, to produce its goals. Polities produce power, not reciprocity; they depend upon authority, not independence; they demand loyalty, not criticism, and seek to exercise coercive, if legitimate, forms of social control. The religious sphere produces salvation, not worldly just deserts; it is premised upon a fundamental inequality, not only between God and merely human believers but between God's representatives - his shepherds - and those they must guide and instruct on earth; and no matter how radically egalitarian or reformed the message, the very transcendental character of religious relationships demands mystery and deference, not reciprocity or dialogue of a transparent kind. In the family, the species is reproduced in a biological and a moral sense; it is organised around eros and love, not self-control and questioning; its organisation depends upon deference in a fundamental way.

Each of these non-civil spheres creates specifically functional kinds of inequalities. Fathers have historically assumed power over women and children in families; property-owners and professional managers organise, lead, and command economic workers; politicians and bureaucrats exercise domination over those who do not hold office in the state; religious notables, whether priests, rabbis, or sheikhs, act imperiously vis-à-vis lay people in their congregations. These privileged accumulations of power may be considered as usurpations, but they are not necessarily so. Certainly it is difficult to conceive how such non-civil spheres could operate in an independent or effective fashion without specialised experts whose authority allowed them to co-ordinate and direct institutional relations - which means, in fact, to 'govern' in some way. It is possible, in fact, to conceive of just and legitimate forms of such inequalities, insofar as the power over goods and process is acquired by persons with distinctive insights and effectively specialised skills.

The problem is that the privileged accumulations in these other spheres, to one degree or another, routinely and systematically become translated into the sphere of civil society itself. So do the particular goods upon which these accumulations of power are based. These goods themselves possess a distinctive charisma, as do the powers that have the authority to speak and act in their name. Money is important, not only because of its instrumental power but also because its possession is typically taken to represent a distinctive and respected achievement in the world of economic life. Grace in the sphere of salvation, patriarchal authority in the family, and power in the political sphere should be understood in similar ways. Yet, as a result of this charisma, these qualities become represented not merely as prestigious possessions acquired in specialised spheres, but as qualities that mean something in civil society itself. Stratification in these other spheres becomes translated into the bifurcating discourse of civil society. To be rich, for example, often seems to suggest moral goodness; insofar is it does, it is translated into the discourse of liberty. To be poor, on the other hand, often exposes one to degradation, to constructions that pollute one in various ways. In one sense this translation is complicated: it involves complex analogical chains between different semiotic codes, metaphorical transformations, and narratives that establish homologous relationships between motives, relations, and institutions in different walks of life. In another sense, the translation is very simple. The privileged accumulations of goods in non-civil spheres are used to achieve power and recognition in civil society, to gain access to its discourse, control over its institutions, and to re-represent the elites of other spheres as ideal participants in the interactive processes of civil life.

I will speak of these boundary relationships in terms of facilitating inputs, destructive intrusions, and civil repairs. Boundary tensions can seriously distort civil society, threatening the very possibility for an effective and democratic social life. These distorting forces are destructive intrusions; in the face of them, civil society can make repairs by seeking to regulate and reform what happens in such non-civil spheres. Yet such subsystem interpenetration can also go the other way. Some of the goods and the social forms produced by other spheres actually facilitate the realisation of a more civil life. Conservative theorists and politicians, not to mention the elites in these noncivil spheres themselves, are inclined to emphasise the facilitating inputs of non-civil spheres to the creation of a good social life. Those on the liberal and radical left are more inclined to emphasise the destructive intrusions that these interpenetrations entail, and the repairs that must be made as a result. Neither side of this argument can be ignored in the effort to theorise civil society in a general way.

That the economic sphere facilitates the construction of a civil society in important ways is an historical and sociological fact that should not be denied. When an economy is structured by markets, behaviour is encouraged that is independent, rational, and self-controlled. It was for this reason that the early intellectuals of capitalism, from Montesquieu to Adam Smith, hailed market societies as a calm and civilising antidote to the militaristic glories of aristocratic life. It is in part for this same reason that societies which have recently exited from Communism have staked their emerging democracies on the construction of market societies. Yet, quite apart from markets, industrialisation itself can be seen in a positive vein. By creating an enormous supply of cheap and widely available material media, mass production lessens the invidious distinctions of status-markers that separated rich and poor in more restricted economies. It becomes increasingly possible for masses of people to express their individuality, their autonomy, and their equality through consumption and, in so doing, to partake of the common symbolic inheritance of cultural life. Facilitating inputs are produced from the production side as well. As Marx himself was among the first to point out, the complex forms of teamwork and co-operation that are demanded in productive enterprises can be considered forms of socialisation, in which persons learn to respect and trust their fellow partners in the civil sphere.

Insofar as the economy supplies the civil sphere with facilities like independence, self-control, rationality, equality, self-realisation, co-operation, and trust, the boundary relation between these two spheres is frictionless, and structural differentiation seems to produce integration and individuation. It must be clear to all but the most die-hard free marketeers, however, that an industrialising, market economy has also thrown roadblocks in the way of the project of civil society. In the everyday language of social science these blockages are expressed purely in terms of economic inequalities, as class divisions, housing differentials, dual labour markets, poverty, and unemployment. These facts only become crystallised in social terms, however, because they are viewed as destructive intrusions into the civil realm. Economic criteria interfere with civil ones.

The stratification of economic products, both human and material, narrows and polarises civil society. It provides a broad field for the discourse of repression, which pollutes and degrades economic failure. Despite the fact that there is no inherent relationship between failure to achieve distinction in the economic realm and failure to sustain expectations in civil society - the lack of connection being the very point of the construction of an independent civil realm - this very connection is continually made. If you are poor you are often thought to be irrational, dependent, and lazy, not only in the economy but in society as such. The relative asymmetry of resources that is inherent in economic life, in other words, becomes translated into projections about civil competence and incompetence. It is often difficult for actors without economic achievement or wealth to communicate effectively in the civil sphere, to receive full respect from its regulatory institutions, or to interact with other, more economically successful, people in a fully civil way. Finally, material power as such, power garnered only in the economic realm, too often becomes an immediate and effective basis for civil claims. Despite the fact that the professionalisation of journalism has separated ownership and effective control, capitalists can buy newspapers, communicative institutions central to civil society, and fundamentally alter their construction of the social scene.

Yet to the degree that civil society exists as an independent force, economically underprivileged actors have dual memberships. They are not only unsuccessful members of the economy; they also have the ability to make claims for respect and power on the basis of their only partially realised membership in the civil realm. On the basis of the implied universalism of solidarity in civil society, moreover, they believe these claims should find a response. They make use of the communicative institutions of civil society, of social movements that demand socialism (or simply economic justice), and of voluntary organisations (such as trade unions) that demand fairness to wage employees. Sometimes they employ their space in civil society to confront economic institutions and elites directly, winning concessions in face-to-face negotiations. At other times, they make use of regulatory institutions, like law and the franchise, to force the state to intervene in economic life on their behalf. While these efforts at repairs often fail, they often succeed in institutionalising 'workers' rights'. Civil criteria now enter directly into the economic sphere. Dangerous working conditions are prohibited; discrimination in labour markets is outlawed; arbitrary economic authority is curtailed; unemployment is controlled and humanised; wealth itself is redistributed according to criteria that are antithetical to those of a strictly economic kind.

Each of the other non-civil spheres has also fundamentally undermined civil society in different times and different ways, especially as they have become intertwined with the segmentations created by time and space. In Catholic countries, Jews and Protestants have often been construed as uncivil and prevented from fully entering civil life. For most of the history of civil societies, patriarchal power in the family has transferred directly into a lack of civil status for women. Scientific and professional power has empowered experts and excluded ordinary persons from full participation in vital civil discussions. Political oligarchies, whether in private organisations or in national governments themselves, have used secrecy and manipulation to deprive members of civil society from access to information about many of the crucial decisions that affect their collective life.

In the course of Western history these intrusions have been so destructive that the social movements organised for repair, and the theorists who articulate their demands, have come to believe that these blockages are intrinsic to civil society itself. Socialists have argued that civil society is essentially and irrevocably bourgeois, that as long as there are markets and private property participants in the economic realm, people can never be treated in a more respectful and egalitarian way. Radical feminists have argued that civil societies are inherently patriarchal, that the very idea of a civil society is impossible to realise in a society that has families which allow men to dominate women. Zionists have argued that European societies are fundamentally anti-semitic. Black nationalists have claimed that racism is essential, and that the civil realm in white settler societies will always, and necessarily, exclude blacks.

In response to these arguments, radical intellectuals, and many of their followers as well, have chosen to exit rather than to exercise voice. They have demanded the construction of an entirely different kind of society, one in which the uncivil nature of the spheres that border civil society would be fundamentally changed. Sometimes these revolutionary demands, and the reactionary efforts to undercut them, have destroyed civil societies. To the degree that national regimes have institutionalised some genuine autonomy for their realms, however, these critics have succeeded not in making revolutions but in creating dramatic reforms. Revolutionary efforts have usually failed, but the claims they have lodged have often succeeded in expanding civil society in highly significant ways. The result, rather than exit, has been the incremental but real integration of formerly excluded groups. This inclusion has not been complete by any means, but it has been substantial nonetheless.

To the degree that there is some institutionalisation of civil society, economic, political, and religious problems are not treated merely - nor sometimes even primarily - as problems within these spheres themselves, but rather as problems of 'our society'. They are treated, both by those making the claims and by those on the receiving end, as deficits in civil society itself, as forces that threaten society's cohesiveness, integrity, morality, and liberty. This is particularly the case because the functional stratification of civil society often merges with the stratification caused by the instantiation of civil society in time and space. Functional problems become intertwined with primordial questions about the capacities generated by race, language, region, timing of arrival, and loyalty to the nation itself. This intertwining makes it even more likely that each of these different kinds of conflicts - functional, spatial, and temporal - will be seen not incidentally but primarily as demands for inclusion into civil society as such. In this situation, inclusion becomes an end in itself, not merely a means of particular repair. Conflicts become struggles for identity and social recognition, for repairing the fragmentation and distortion of civil society self.

This contribution is an extract from a larger project the author has been working on, entitled 'Possibilities of Justice - Civil Society and Its Contradictions'.

Civil society and violence

A critique of John Keane

Robert Fine

Robert Fine *takes issue with 'neat' ideas of civil society. In particular he criticises John Keane's work for avoiding any conceptualisation of the intrinsic relationships that exist between civil society and violence.*

Civil society theory is a loosely defined and diverse set of approaches which emerged in the 1980s, and was closely identified with struggles in Central and East Europe against the Soviet Union and Empire. Its distinguishing mark was to privilege civil society over other spheres of social and political life, on the ground that it is civil society that furnishes the fundamental conditions of liberty in the modern world. The mission of civil society theory is to defend civil society from the forces which beset and threaten to colonise it: on one side, the power of the political state; on the other, the economic power of capital.

The concept of civil society was used to indicate a 'third road' - one that is neither utopian socialism nor utopian capitalism but the life-world of the middle. In political-geographic terms civil society was conceived as neither east nor west, neither Americanism nor Russianism, neither free market nor state planning, but rather central European. Civil society was placed on the side of agency, creativity, activity, productivity, freedom, association and life itself. The economic and political systems were depicted in essentially negative terms: conformity, consumerism, passivity, privatisation, coercion, determination, necessity, etc. Through this opposition between life and death, activity and passivity, agency and structure, communication and violence, civil society theory justified the primacy of civil society over the political and economic spheres. It elevated civil society as a special domain - one which not only had to be recognised but also nurtured and protected from the prevailing forces of modern technology and instrumental rationality. Civil society theory was not just a theory of civil society, but a theory which in some sense classed civil society above the other spheres of modernity.

One of the central claims of civil society theory is that civil society is a sphere of social life in which violence is either actually or at least potentially absent - that civil society begins where violence ends. This conception was born on the borderlines of the descriptive and the normative. As Adam Michnik put it, the idea of civil society was not to separate people into 'maggots and angels' but to create the possibility of a 'civilised conversation' based on the recognition of difference, respect for political argument, and the construction not only of a legal and institutional structure of rights but above all of a 'real community of free individuals, created anew each day'.

One of Britain's leading protagonists of civil society theory, John Keane, reflects this view in his work, particularly in *Reflections on Violence* (published by Verso in 1996). He argues that civil society is in principle a sphere of non-violence and that it acts as an antidote to the violence both of unrestricted private property and of the state. He depicts civil society as a complex, dynamic, well-regulated community that is devoid of violence and based on a principle of choice (p11). He maintains that violence is fundamentally incompatible with civil society rules of solidarity, liberty and equality and that violence and civil society cannot co-exist (p70). Keane turns this opposition almost into a matter of definition when he states that 'if violence begins to plague the subjects of any civil society, then that ensemble of non-state institutions passes over into the category of an uncivil society'(p71). He argues that externally civil society is against war because war is bad for business (p154); and that internally civil society is against repression because market economies are dependent on 'a dense and delicate forest of non-violent civil institutions' (p155).

There is, however, more than a hint of ambivalence in Keane's discussion. He acknowledges the 'chronic persistence of violence within all extant civil societies' (p22) and the fact that 'all known forms of civil society are plagued by endogenous sources of incivility' (p63). He recognises that the potential for civil society to pass over into 'uncivil societies' is always already present. In the face of this difficulty, Keane reformulates the relation between non-violence and civil society as one of 'elective affinity' rather than of an 'absolute bond' (p91). He sees a 'troubling contradiction' in the fact that on the one hand violence is the antithesis of civil society and on the other 'every known form of civil society tends to produce the same violent antithesis' (p107). Keane also recognises that violence does not only enter into civil societies from without but also that civil societies generate 'from within their own structures patterns of violence that contradict the freedom, solidarity and civility which otherwise make them so attractive' (p114). For example, they promote violence by enabling certain groups to 'organise for the pursuit of wealth and power' and by providing 'handsome opportunities for certain power groups tempted by the dream of expansionism' (p114). At the extreme, civil societies may be 'twisted and deformed into grotesque shapes' by gun-wielding gangs and cartels which arise from within civil society, and may even give rise to local uncivil wars conducted by genocidal killers who have 'emptied themselves of all thought and morals' (p140) - wars which abolish the distinction between war and crime and turn civil society into a maelstrom of 'destruction and self-destruction' (p141). Keane writes that such uncivil wars are the unwanted progeny of what happens when people 'ransack the legal monopoly of armed force long claimed by states' (p141) and re-appropriate it for civil society.

W e are faced by a real difficulty. On the one hand, we are presented with an idealised conception of the non-violence of civil society; on the other, by the extremes of endogenous violence which tear civil society apart. Is it feasible to resolve this troubling contradiction? How can we square the circle? Keane offers his own set of distinctions between what he considers to be legitimate and illegitimate forms of violence. He argues that violence is legitimate when its purpose is the creation or strengthening of a pluralistic, non-violent civil society (p91), or when it resists the destruction of a pluralistic, non-violent civil society (for example, the Warsaw ghetto uprising against Nazi occupation), or when it is the product of a community of 'thinking, judging, acting citizens' who are eager to work for a civil society (p107) and who feel shame for 'what we have done to each other during this long century of violence' (p185). Violence is illegitimate when it takes the form of 'genocidal wars, fire-bombed cities, nuclear explosions, concentration camps, or orgies of private blood-letting' (p185), or when violence is glorified as a cult of violence, or when it is justified according to some dialectical acrobatics which has faith, for example, that 'lumpenproletarian and proletarian mugging and murder would give way to the organised militancy of the working class' (p113). Keane appeals to the faculty of judgement and wise political thinking in order to sail between the Scylla of celebrating violence and the Charybdis of total pacifism.

Few would argue with this contrast between, for instance, the violence of Nazi occupation and that of Jewish resistance, though the morality of Jewish non-resistance against the Nazis raises thornier issues and has been widely debated. There is perhaps a greater danger in legitimising violence simply on the grounds that it aims at the creation of a loosely defined civil society - since it might appear to offer a *carte blanche* for western armed interventions in contexts where a civil society is deemed not to exist. Once it is admitted that civil society contains its own autochthonous sources of violence, it is difficult to turn it into an absolute standard of legitimacy. Keane sees a civil society remedy for violence in the cultivation of 'public spheres of controversy' in which the violent exercise of power is monitored non-violently by citizens (p165). He favours the development of public spheres which include everything from rap music and the women's movement to CNN, the *New York Times* and public broadcasting. He casts aside criticisms of the media - as advanced by, for example, Baudrillard - which portray the media as serving up massacres as mass entertainment, and he finds hope in the beneficial effects of other television images: the joy of seeing 'the first green shoots of civil society' arise within uncivil war zones, or the shame which arises within us when we hear the crying of those who have been violated (p182). Following Hannah Arendt, Keane aims to rediscover 'the Greek conviction that public life and violence had nothing in common' (p166); but the difficulty is that his own representation of civil society includes images of mindless, instinctual, brutish and shameless violence and ends up with a frightening image of those 'who simply want to kill' (p90). To my mind, this brief discussion of John Keane's reflections on violence shows how difficult it is to understand the relation between civil society and violence once we start off with the philosophical presuppositions of civil society theory and its presumption of the innocence of civil society.

The great strength of civil society theory is to defend the idea of a free body of citizens based on the associational life of civil society, representative institutions and the rule of law, against the external power of the state; against those who treat the state as a secular deity whose claims upon its citizens are always unquestionable and irresistible; and against an *étatisme* which declares that the state must impose order on civil society by means of police, prisons, executive, crown and other administrative organs. Civil society theory posits the autonomous generation of solidarity and identity by means of a system of right, the associations of civil society, their representatives in the state parliament and public opinion.[1] It recognises that citizens have only a restricted part to play in the business of

> 'the task of social theory is not to idealise civil society but to understand its nature'

the existing state, and that it is essential to provide people with activity of a general character over and above their private business. It derives the category of 'civil society' from liberal thought in such a way that, instead of restricting public life to the single level of the political state, a series of levels are given key roles to play, including 'the public rights of private persons, the publicity of legal processes, the public life of autonomous associations, and the interaction between public opinion and the deliberations of the legislature' (Arato, p318). Civil society theory expands rights of participation beyond anything envisaged in classical republicanism either in its Lockeian or Rousseauian variants. It goes beyond the liberal values of civil society seen merely as a de-politicised sphere of atomised individuals, and looks to a comprehensive public and political life beyond the official political institutions of government. And it also goes beyond those who say that civil society is merely a fraud - a façade for hidden forms of domination and exploitation masquerading as a benign, neutral or natural order. As Ernest Gellner put it in his *Conditions of Liberty* (Penguin 1994), as a slogan taken out of the history of enlightenment thought, civil society was and remains a 'shining emblem'. Its commitment is to a plurality of institutions and ideas strong enough to prevent the establishment of any monopoly of power and truth and to counterbalance the power of the state.

However, if we accept that civil society is a distinct sphere of modern social

---

1. See for example Andrew Arato's essay in Cornell's edited collection, *Hegel and Legal Theory*.

life, then the task of social theory is not to idealise this form of society but to understand its nature and location within modern social life as a whole - including the types of violence which it generates. Civil society is the distinctive achievement of the modern age, which for the first time in human history provides institutional support for autonomous individuality. It is the sphere in which, as Hegel once put it in his *Philosophy of Right*, 'all individual characteristics are liberated'; but it is also a 'system of all-round interdependence', in which the subsistence, welfare and rights of individuals are interwoven with and grounded on the subsistence, welfare and rights of all (see the CUP 1991 edition, §183). As a system of needs, the universality of civil society can only be abstract because individuals are private persons who have their own interest as their end. They regard society, the universal, as something hostile and prejudicial to their own ends. They try to keep it at a distance and they imagine that they can do without it, even though in fact the satisfaction of their own ends cannot be satisfied without society. Civil society is a form of society that is, as Hegel put it, 'lost in extremes'. On the one hand, it results in the endless multiplication of needs and of the means of satisfying them. On the other, it ends in an equally infinite increase in dependency and want. It affords a spectacle of both extravagance and misery, as well as of the physical and moral corruption that can accompany both. It gives rise to an excess both of wealth and poverty, and can find no other solution to the latter than to offer charity, or leave the poor to their fate, or direct them to beg from the public. It was the social question raised by the rise of civil society that led enlightenment thought to look to state intervention as a necessity, and to appreciate the violence that is endemic within civil society itself. If civil society was a sphere of 'difference', held together by the hidden hand of the market but also torn apart by extremes of wealth and poverty, the state appeared as the sphere of unity invested with the task not merely of guaranteeing property but of embodying human values. The illusion behind the enlightenment view of the state should not blind us to its insight into the character of civil society.

Civil society is a modern society in which individuals enter the social stage as owners of property - even if it is only their own bodies or capacity for labour - and pursue their own private interests in a network of relations mediated by the exchange of commodities and contractual relations between property owners. It is a complex and differentiated sphere of social life, incorporating and linking together a system of needs, a system of rights, a system of welfare and a network of free associations concerned with their own collective interests, or the welfare of others, or the attainment of certain social goals (like nuclear disarmament or the stoppage of war), or even the general administration of society (like political parties). Situated between the family and the state, civil society is host to both culture and barbarism. We are free, of course, to define violence out of civil society by the simple act of declaring that where violence starts, civil society ends and becomes uncivil. But this definitional exercise does not help us understand the sources of the violence which marks and mars our own age - whether it is the displacement of wars between states by 'uncivil wars' between ethnically or religiously defined groupings within civil society, or the displacement of state law by the gangster 'law' of rival armed syndicates imposing their own type of 'popular justice'.

I f we accept Weber's proposition that the state attempts to monopolise the legitimate means of violence, this does not exclude the exercise of other (illegitimate) forms of violence in civil society, nor the failure of the state's attempt at monopoly. Let us not forget Herbert Marcuse's insight into the relation between fascism and the idea of the modern state. In the latter it is the rational state which rules civil society; in fascism it is civil society (or rather the most powerful economic and political forces in civil society) that rules the state. Weber reveals the pivotal importance of the state in expropriating the means of violence from civil society and regulating its exercise, as well as the means of violence which can accumulate in civil society once the state, for one reason or another, fails to perform this appropriate function. All of which is to say that we should not be misled by those appearances which suggest that the state is essentially a site of violence and civil society is essentially the site of its absence. There is no sphere in the modern system of 'right' which is exempt from the forces which beset the system as a whole.

I am suggesting that it is an illusion to associate civil society with non-violence and that there is danger in this illusion. The danger, as I see it, is this. If civil society is ideally treated as a non-violent community, and yet it is empirically self-evident that civil society in fact generates its own endogenous sources of violence between rival interests, then the search is on for those who are deemed responsible for this corruption or distortion. In other words, my contention is that the idealisation of civil society breeds *ressentiment* against those who are to be blamed for the shadow that falls between its image and its actuality. A brief survey of civil society theory will reveal various alleged culprits.

One often cited culprit is Marx or the Marxist. For example, when Keane in an earlier article on 'remembering the dead' called for a return to the lost treasures of enlightenment thought, the reverse side of this medal was the call to 'forget Marx'. It was as if Marxism was responsible for the decline and fall of the idea of civil society, because Marx stood either for the total subsumption of civil society to the state or for the total subsumption of the state to civil society. Either way the balance between state and civil society was destroyed: in the first case through state despotism and in the second through party despotism. These apparently opposite errors came together, according to Keane, in the form of the totalitarian Party-State.

Another culprit is the figure of the nationalist. The nationalist is presented as a most uncivil beast: a scavenger who feeds upon a pre-existing sense of nationhood, a destroyer of heterogeneity who squeezes the nation into the Nation, a shameless ideologue driven by a bovine will to simplify things, a purveyor of blame who supposes that only foreigners and enemies of the nation are guilty, a bigot who portrays the Other as inferior rubbish. In this way, Keane turns the 'nationalist' into the quintessential bearer of violence in the modern age, at the same time as he reserves the concept of 'national identity' for that civic sense of national belonging of which he approves. The problem here does not lie in the making of distinctions between national identity and nationalism, or between civil and ethnic nationalism, but rather in putting all that is non-violent or legitimately-violent on the side of one and all that is illegitimately violent on the side of the other. A polarity which offers such blanket condemnation of those held guilty for the corruption of civil society - 'emptied ... of all thought and morals ... they simply want to kill' - also allows no challenge to 'our own' claims to innocence.

Sometimes it is the politician who is held to be the culprit. If the only legitimate role of the politician is that of defending and refining the rules of the game of civil society, then responsibility for its corruption lies with the politician who oversteps his mark. The politician only loves power, and conversely power loves politicians. Thus from the point of view of proselytisers of civil society, it could be argued that the less power a politician has, the better. Hitler appears as the extreme paradigm of the politician's trade, and no matter what ideology the politician appeals to, it is held that what s/he says is only a means of gaining power.

My belief is that the scapegoating of the Marxist, the nationalist, the mindless murderer, the politician - all blamed for the failure of civil society to actualise its non-violent potential - flows from a failure to see the violence of civil society itself. It seems to me that the most telling analysis of this tendency came from Marx himself when he explored the scapegoating of the Jew by the German socialist, Bruno Bauer, who argued that Jews were not worthy of equal rights until they first gave up their Judaism (in 'On the Jewish Question'). I share Marx's basic argument, that Bauer failed to see the violence inherent in the modern split between civil society and the state - and he failed to see that in the former the pursuit of money had become a 'world power'; and because of this he attributed to the Jews in particular the negative, alien, egoistic, materialistic, civil society-destroying qualities of the 'moneyman'.

Marx argued that Judaism reaches its peak with the completion of civil society, but civil society first reaches its completion in the Christian world. Only under the rule of Christianity, which makes all national, natural, moral and theoretical relationships external to man, could civil society separate itself completely from political life, tear apart all the species-bonds of man, substitute egoism and self need for those bonds, and dissolve the human world into a world of atomistic individuals confronting each other in enmity.

The young Marx did not at this stage of his writing understand the social dimension of civil society - tending instead to cast it onto the abstract political community of the state - but what he did understand is that Bauer's socialist anti-semitism represented the civil society theory of fools.

Today civil society theory expresses the very antithesis of the intolerance to Jews which Bauer stood for. But if I am right in my analysis, the stress on an ideal, non-violent community could open all the wrong doors.

Narrating evil
Moral theory as a bridge between the aesthetic and the moral
María Pía Lara

Maria Pia Lara *asks how the uncivil - evil - dimensions of society can be represented through narratives.*

During the twentieth century the invention of gas chambers, death camps, and a multitude of techniques to serve state policies of genocide and terrorism, together with the brain-washing techniques of panoptical control, has created a space in which the cruel features of our times can seem to feature as their signature. Pessimistic theories have reflected on the signature of our age as being something unavoidable, necessary, or contingently produced by the selfish and cruel drives of humankind. This is not a novel way of thinking about human beings and politics. Since Hobbes, there have been political theories that have dealt with the darkest sides of our behaviour, but they have done so in order to justify specific features of their theories that end up by conceptualising humans and their actions in a simplistic and one-sided way. As Habermas has argued:

> from Horkheimer and Adorno to Baudrillard and Zygmunt Bauman, from Heidegger to Foucault and Derrida, the totalitarian features of the age have left their mark on the very structure of its diagnosis. But, in spite of their illuminating power, these negativistic interpretations allow themselves to be carried away by the horror images and fail to see the reverse side of disaster.[1]

1. J. Habermas, 'Learning by Disaster? A Diagnosis', *Constellations* Vol.5, No. 3, 1998, p312.

Recently, theorists of democracy have started to focus on the possibility of understanding our societies not only in a one-sided way, either positively or negatively, but from both sides, by clarifying the dynamics of human behaviour through theories based on complexity and the contradictory features of human interaction. Jeffrey C. Alexander has been a pioneer in this field, since in his most recent work he has defined civil society as allowing civic spaces for solidarity, while at the same time acknowledging the exclusionary sides of that society, as the uncivil dimensions; this allows us to conceptualise society and its struggles as spaces of conflict and complexity.[2] In the same way, it is important to focus now on what it was that made the last century such an extensive display of cruelty and violence, making those 'evil' actions the signature of our age. It is in this sense that we are obliged to go back in history and to reflect on the problem of evil, as Hannah Arendt once thought we should do. Hannah Arendt thought that the problem of evil would be a 'fundamental' question of post-war intellectual life in Europe'.[3] However, intellectuals in postwar Europe and the US became more concerned with a new kind of fragmentation, a dark backdrop for democracy, one announcing a new split for Europe in the cold war years. But the problem of evil was one of Arendt's main interests in her own political thinking, and the culture of the postwar years reflected concerns with evil through narratives in novels, stories, films, and TV shows. It is only now, at the end of the century, that it seems important to go back and revise our recent history in terms of conceptualising evil. After all, as Bernstein says, we are in 'a century that future generations may label "the Age of Genocides"' (p128). Evil has become an unavoidable moral and political problem because of the historical events of our past, the Holocaust, the massive killing fields of Cambodia, the ethnic cleansing of the Muslims of Srebrenice and Kosovo and the bloody dictatorships of Latin America where people were banished from the earth. This shift in emphasis towards an interest in evil as part of the uncivil side of civil societies should open a path towards what I like to call the moral grounds for a new consciousness, a stage for 'moral learning'.

Evil cannot be conceived as an abstract term. It is also absurd to view it as

---

2. See his essay in this issue, and his forthcoming book *Possibilities of Justice*.
3. R. Bernstein, 'Did Hannah Arendt Change Her Mind? From Radical Evil to the Banality of Evil' in *Hannah Arendt. Twenty Years Later*, L. May and J. Kohn (eds), MIT Press 1996, p127.

a set of formulas describing specific behaviours or the lack of moral concern in them. Conceptualising evil seems to be a complicated issue, one that still remains a huge challenge for philosophy. I want to argue that, in order to be able to say something about evil from a philosophical point of view, we need narratives. But we also need to develop a 'normative bridge' that can give us some conceptual understanding of the mediating processes that operate between the full expression of those narratives and the moral effect that occurs in the spectator or reader once we reappropriate such experiences. In order to do that, I want to go back to Hannah Arendt.

It was Hannah Arendt who first conceived of storytelling as related to political and moral affairs. She believed that the meaning that a story provides could help us understand the complexity and uniqueness of all human action, and, at the same time, that the role of storytelling could become a process of moral learning through 'reflexive' judgement. Today, narrations have become instrumental tools for social theory, anthropology, and even law. Stories provide moral meanings that capture the experience of suffering and simultaneously help to build up a collective memory. 'It has seldom been realised that the listener's naïve relationship to the storyteller is controlled by his interest in retaining what he is told', says Benjamin: 'The cardinal point for the unaffected listener is to assure himself of the possibility of reproducing the story. Memory is the epic faculty *par excellence*'.[4] It is this interconnection between experiences as sufferings and the memory of actions created by recollection that gives storytelling its privileged place in a theory about evil. That is why Arendt's conception of storytelling is especially relevant in regard to the problem of evil. And it is in the interconnection of evil to storytelling that I wish to develop my own theory of 'postmetaphysical reflexive judgement'. I want to argue that storytelling is a necessary tool for providing a moral frame for thinking about evil; however, because storytelling leaves the reader or the spectator with the job of drawing implications from the story, it is important to describe normatively - that is philosophically - the specifically moral implications of the narrative and the way in which they help to formulate a post-metaphysical theory of reflexive judgement. It is this explicit exercise which I will call narrating evil

---

4. W. Benjamin, 'The Storyteller. Reflections on the Works of Nikolai Leskov', in *Illuminations. Essays and Reflections*, Hannah Arendt (ed), Schocken Books 1968.

through 'reflexive judgement', a Kantian term that Arendt used in her own original sense. In this essay I will first formulate the elements that are contained in storytelling and argue for their relevance in moral terms; second, I will reappraise these elements by showing how they become connected with the act of remembrance that clarifies the normative sphere.

Storytelling and judging evil

Arendt's notion of storytelling has recently been the subject of many studies, precisely because she had the idea of bringing it to the territory of political and moral spheres. Thus, Lisa Jane Disch writes that 'storytelling is the term Arendt uses to describe critical understanding from experience'.[5] Storytellers make us re-experience the past through narration, and as Disch argues, it is 'in the form of suffering by memory operating retrospectively and perceptively' (p100) that we are able to reconcile ourselves and liberate ourselves from the 'deeds' of the past. ('Forgiveness, in other words, is not a divine gift but a political act of releasing other human beings from the "deeds of the past"', p101.) Perhaps what makes Arendt the perfect theorist for narrating and evil is her conceptual link of narratives to history and time.

Arendt had a conception of time similar to that of Walter Benjamin; it is a conception that connects the past with the future. We need to go back to the past, to the sufferers; we owe it to them in order to build up a future, to begin anew. While Arendt worked on developing a secular conception of time, she sewed together Augustine's conception with those of Heidegger and Benjamin, giving them a forceful new moral interpretation. History also became one of Arendt's main concerns. Arendt was against the idea of progress and, because she believed in the possibility of freedom, she rejected the idea that history was a 'rational' force of humanity. When weaving time into history, Arendt stumbled on her most interesting scenario, finding that storytelling and judgement are tied together in the understanding of evil as unique phenomena of the twentieth century. Seyla Benhabib finds in this part of Arendt's work four distinctive themes: 'historicisation and salvation; the exercise of empathy, imagination, and historical judgement; the pitfalls of analogical thinking; and the moral resonance of narrative language.[6] Arendt's

---

5. L. J. Disch, *Hannah Arendt and the Limits of Philosophy*, Cornell University Press 1994, p107.
6. S. Benhabib, *The Reluctant Modernism of Hannah Arendt*, Sage 1996, p87.

conception of secular redemption through narratives about the past is the way she coped with the present. In doing so, she offers us a model of how to build up a new beginning - for narrative understanding can itself become an act of moral judgement.

Once we understand Arendt's concern with judgement and narration, it becomes clear that a 'historical narrator' recreates a shared reality from the standpoint of all concerned. And as Martha Nussbaum has argued, 'storytelling and literary imagining are not opposed to rational argument, but can provide essential ingredients in rational arguments'.[7] Stories about evil are important because the kinds of arguments they provide allow them to become a territory of self-reflection, of interpretation and of understanding. They become a part of our *own* experience. Walter Benjamin knew this capacity very well, and he explains why is it that Herodotus became the first Greek storyteller: 'A story is different. It does not expand itself. It preserves and concentrates its strength and is capable of releasing it even after a long time'. Benjamin refers to Montaigne's famous account of Herodotus's story about the Egyptian king: 'Montaigne asked himself why the king mourned only when he caught sight of his servant. Montaigne answers: "Since he was already overfull of grief, it took only the smallest increase for it to burst through its dams"'. But one could also say, according to Benjamin, 'The king is not moved by the fate of those of royal blood, for it is his own fate. Or: We are moved by much on the stage that does not move us in real life; to the king, this servant is only an actor. Or: Great grief is pent up and breaks forth only with relaxation'. Herodotus offers no explanation because he was, according to Benjamin, the first storyteller: 'His report is the driest. That is why this story from ancient Egypt is still capable after thousands of years of arousing astonishment and thoughtfulness. It resembles the seeds of grain which have lain for centuries in the chambers of the pyramids shut up air-tight and have retained their germinative power to this day' ('The Storyteller', p90). What Benjamin is referring to here is the power of the story to move us into the moral realm of interpretation and to a different kind of understanding of human affairs, one that has to do with appropriating experiences from others in the same act as judging them - which liberates us from the burdens of the past. Here then,

---

7.   In *Poetic Justice. The Literary Imagination and Public Life*, Beacon Press 1995.

appropriation means also being able to think in terms of 'exemplary validity', a term that Arendt took from Kant, and of which she said:

> Kant accords to examples the same role in judgements that the intuitions called schemata have for experience and cognition. Examples play a role in both reflective and determinate judgements, that is whenever we are concerned with particulars. In *The Critique of Judgement*, i.e., in the treatment of reflexive judgements, where one does not subsume a particular under a concept, the example helps one in the same way in which the schema helped one to recognise the table as table. The examples lead and guide us, and the judgement thus acquires 'exemplary validity'. [8]

Storytelling thus entails finding a 'true' language. By creating a specific language that will describe certain actions as cases of 'exemplary validity', the storyteller provides for a new meaning of old terms - in our case, for a wider understanding of the process by which evil actions reorder our own language, resignifying our everyday understanding into something different. In the Germany of the 1930s and 1940s the word 'Jews' became a description of non-human, a group that concentrated all otherness away from humanity. Symbolic events that were named then, like '*Kristallnacht*', are understood by contemporary stories as clear descriptions of stages of horror. Terms like '*Judenrate*', '*concentration camps*', '*extermination*', '*final solution*' were resignified in the stories written after the war ended, once people outside the perpetrators started to publicly learn about those facts.

In these forms, it is possible to see Arendt herself as a storyteller, and to describe her efforts to create a new language for narrating evil as the starting point for a new postmetaphysical theory. Arendt reworked the terms 'radical evil', 'absolute evil', and the 'banality of evil'; and gave new meanings to our traditional understanding by expressing clearly that 'it is inherent in our entire philosophical tradition that we cannot conceive of a "radical evil" and this is true both for Christian theology, which conceded even to the Devil himself a celestial origin, as well as for Kant.' Kant was 'the only philosopher who, in the

---

8. H. Arendt, ed. Ronald Beiner, *Lectures on Kant's Political Philosophy*, University of Chicago Press 1982, p84.

word he coined for it [evil], at least must have suspected the existence of this evil even though he immediately rationalised it in the concept of a "perverted ill will" that could be explained by comprehensible motives'. Arendt asserted, 'we actually have nothing to fall back on in order to understand a phenomenon that nevertheless confronts us with its overpowering reality and breaks down all standards we know. There is only one thing that seems to be discernible: we may say that radical evil has emerged in connection with a system in which all men have become equally superfluous'.[9] This understanding of the unique operation performed by one group of men against another later led Arendt to accept the invitation to become a witness of Eichmann's trial, and it was there in Jerusalem that she realised how the evil that she had described earlier - as stripping away the essential features of humanity - was caused by shallowness and rigidity, in fact, by what she conceptualised as an 'exemplary case' of the 'banality of evil'. Arendt created her own vocabulary that described two different stages in the understanding of the stories about the Holocaust. In *The Origins of Totalitarianism* she narrated what happened to humans qua humans as the sequences of terror stripping away individual identity. In *Eichmann in Jerusalem,* she portrayed one of the perpetrators of what she thought was the darkest action of all times, and found that he had no comprehension of the moral meaning of his crime.

Much has been written about these philosophical stories, and I do not want to insist again on the fact that there are many different interpretations of them. I am interested in making explicit the ways in which evil can be conceptualised through narrations that either capture 'evil' through the process of making evident the resignifying processes of words that describe evil actions, or - as in the case we just saw of Arendt herself - create a new vocabulary to describe the 'exemplary validity' of evil actions. Some narrations belong to the first group and could be considered narrations that recollect other stories and configure an effort to bring these experiences to light; there are some stories, however, that fictionalise and develop our understanding of evil through creating symbolic configurations that help us grasp some of evil's other sides.

In relation to the first group, we can cite a book about evil called *A Lexicon*

---

9.   H. Arendt, *The Origins of Totalitarianism*, Harcourt Brace Jovanovich 1975, p459.

of Terror. Argentina and the Legacies of Torture, written by Marguerite Feitlowitz (OUP 1998). Feitlowitz explains that her book deals with 'the languages of terror - texts and subtexts, high rhetoric, dialects, and patois'(p ix); through this she calls our attention to the way in which 'missing' came to be a term that described a group of people, 30,000 approximately, who disappeared from the earth without leaving a trace; suspected 'subversives' were kidnapped from the streets, tortured in secret concentration camps, and 'disappeared'.

In the second group we could cite novels like *Doktor Faustus* by Thomas Mann, and the film script *Death and the Maiden* by Ariel Dorfman, which was made as a movie by Roman Polanski. Mann deals with the Nazi *zeitgeist*. His artist, Adrian Leverkühn, was ready to give up everything for a perfect musical work, which he achieved at the price of never being able to love again - he was stripped of his soul. For Mann, the expression of the times were exactly how humanity lost its soul.

On the other hand, Dorfman's story is about torture as an indelible memory, which hunts those who have suffered from it and impedes them from living any kind of normal life ever again. His story goes further than that, for his heroine will search for vengeance because of her crippled sense of identity and the nightmare in which she is immersed, and from which she cannot awaken. But what Dorfman captures best is the sense of how the cruelty of torture is a permanent damage in a person's life, how there is no way to escape such an evil.

To conclude, let me briefly focus on some recent work that aims to study and decode the meanings of evil in religious narratives. In *The Curse of Cain. The Violent Legacy of Monotheism* (University of Chicago Press 1997), Regina M. Schwartz argues that the narratives of the bible have become 'the foundation of a prevailing understanding of ethnic, religious, and national identity as defined negatively, over against others. We are "us" because we are not "them" (p x). Her study of these biblical narratives locates the origin of violence in 'identity formations', for 'as forms of violence' they encode 'Western culture's central myth of collective identity'(p6). She offers compelling evidence that biblical narratives have shaped the concept of nationalism and, further, that 'throughout all this reading and interpreting, German versions of biblical narratives of collective identity assumed their place in conceiving modern nationalism'(p11).

In *The Origin of Satan* (Vintage 1995), Elaine Pagels focuses on the Gospels to deconstruct the meaning of Satan, arguing that those biblical texts functioned 'to confirm for Christians their own identification with God and to demonise their opponents - first other Jews, then pagans, and later dissident Christians called heretics' (p xvii). Like Schwartz, Pagels understands that the symbolic figure of 'Satan' played a major role in configuring new identities. This time, however, it is Christians who developed their ideas about Satan as a 'way of characterising one's actual enemies as the embodiment of transcendent forces' (p13), and the story of Jesus as narrated in the Gospels becomes the story of God's struggle against Satan. Such narratives blame Jewish enemies and minimise the role that the Romans played in the killing of Jesus. Pagels's fascinating book goes on to show how the Gospels remove the meaning of old stories: 'Many scholars have noted these parallels between Jesus, Moses, and Israel. But no one, so far as I know, has observed that Mathew reverses the traditional roles, casting the Jewish king, Herod, in the villain's role traditionally reserved for Pharaoh. Through this device he turns the alien enemies of Israel's antiquity into the intimate enemies, as Mathew perceives them'(p79). Thus Pagels provides for a cultural reading of the gospel narratives, so that we can trace the origins of 'anti-semitism' in the symbolic configuration of 'the Jews' as 'human evil'(p104).

Pagels's narrative of the Gospels not only offers us empirical and theoretical evidence of how one can grasp the 'meanings' of evil as it relates to racism, ethnic cleansing and contemporary hatred. It also serves the symbolic purpose of configuring our consciousness so that we can regain our critical judgement. It is precisely this link that makes storytellers so precious for narrating evil from a normative philosophical point of view.

Towards a European civil society?

William Outhwaite

William Outhwaite explores the possibilities for the development of a European civil society, and the problems and promises that this might involve.

Contemporary Europe might seem a particularly crass example of the uncivil dimensions of civil society: a European society which is not (or not yet) one, racked by resentments resulting from colonialism and its end, from state socialism and its end, and from the rise of new economic and political powers elsewhere in the world. Much of Europe is torn apart by national conflicts, while most of its more prosperous states have been shoehorned by small numbers of enthusiasts into a partial federation which is notionally presided over by an unloved political and administrative bureaucracy and which has set up a Fortress Europe against cheap food and poor people. This may indeed still look like a 'dark continent'. On the other hand, of course, one cannot forget that the concept and the political theory of civil society are an invention of Europe and of European settler colonies, and that these were substantially advanced between the late 1960s and the early 1990s, particularly in the 1980s by Eastern European dissidents; moreover Europe, despite everything, is currently in the forefront of postnational democratic integration.

In this essay I shall be looking at the brighter side of the European picture, and asking in particular how far one can discern the beginnings of a European civil society which is more than just the sum of civil societies in Europe. In a value choice which I shall not justify here, but am of course willing to defend in subsequent discussion, I am assuming that something of this kind is desirable - that, to paraphrase Willy Brandt in a different context, what belongs together should grow together. And since Europe is anyway embarked on an integration process, for better or worse, it can at least be argued that this requires some sort of civil society dimension.

I am also making the theoretical assumption that, despite all the vicissitudes of the concept of civil society (by which I mean associational life at a variety of levels and shading off into conceptions of the public sphere), and of the reality of civil society politics, one can meaningfully talk about the existence of civil societies, however embattled, in most if not all of Europe. Whether there is also an emergent European civil society is a further question, which I shall address indirectly, in a sort of pincer movement, via some remarks about European identities on the one hand and European-level institutions and practices on the other. A discussion of European civil society, I think, necessarily hangs between these two poles. My approach is therefore something like that advanced by Habermas in 1974 in an early reflection on the possibilities of social identities not tied to territorial states and their membership.[1] A collective identity, Habermas argues, can only be conceived in a reflexive form, in an awareness that one has opportunities to participate in processes of communication in which identity formation occurs as a continuous learning process. Such value and norm creating communications by no means always have the precison of discourses, and they are by no means always institutionalised and therefore to be expected at particular times and places. They often remain diffuse, appear under very different definitions and flow out of the 'base' into the pores of organisationally structured areas of life. They have a subpolitical character, i.e. they operate below the level of political decision processes, but they indirectly influence the political system because they change the normative framework of political decisions (p116).

Habermas has of course turned more recently to address the issue of postnational and in particular European identities and formations in more detail. Gerard Delanty's work adopts a similar approach.

---

1. J. Habermas, 'Können komplexe Gesellschaften eine vernünftige Identität ausbilden?', in *Zur Rekonstrutktion des historischen Materialismus*, Suhrkamp 1976.

I think, then, that to talk of a European civil society presupposes some sort of affirmative answer to similar questions about the existence of some minimal version of a European identity, perhaps a cultural identity. As Reinhold Viehoff and Rien Segers put it, in the introduction to their edited collection on this theme, many of the conflicts accompanying the European integration process have a cultural content, wherever they may formally be located in institutional structures.[2] At the same time, however, to frame the question of civil society in this way raises the stakes since, as Klaus Eder points out in the same collection (p149), to start from the premise that there should be some sort of European identity and to look for ways of adequately representing it is 'to turn the logic of collective identity formation on its head'. Nevertheless, Eder insists, if it is to be more than an instrumental association of nation states dressed up as a 'community', 'Europe needs culture in order to found a transnational order on a consensus' (pp152-3). This is the case even if, as he goes on to stress, this may be as much as anything a consensus on how to handle conflicts.

What can be said, first, about the residual distinctiveness of Europe as a cultural region of the modern world? A familiar theme, invoked even in an advertising series by Shell some ten years ago, is diversity, notably the diversity of languages. Compared to the largely anglophone societies of North America or the area sharing Chinese pictograms, or even large regions such as India or the former USSR with an established lingua franca, Europe looks rather a mess. It is at least true that in the European case a pattern of linguistic variation largely coexisting with the boundaries of developed modern states creates powerful entrenched structures and interests which in turn, act as obstacles to cultural and political integration. (It is obvious, at least to this particular English-speaker, that the official language of the European Union ought to be English, just as it is obvious that its principal institutions should all be centralised in Brussels, but no-one quite dares to say so.) This, then, if it is a distinctive feature of European culture, is one which is centrifugal rather than centripetal.

Europe's position as a major cultural producer is of course one of the effects of its previous world hegemony, partly preserved in that of its world languages:

---

2. R Viehoff and R. T. Segers, *Kultur, Identität, Europa*, Suhrkamp 1999, p28

English, French, Spanish, Portuguese and to some extent even Dutch. Again, this is both a source of division, as competition intensifies worldwide between the British Councils, Goethe-Institute, Alliances Françaises, Istituti Italiani and so on, but this diversity may also be a source of strength. European culture has also stood up well in many ways to the challenge of North American imports. This applies not just to cultural commodities such as films but also to material aspects of life such as the car-based civilisation; despite everything, most European cities remain less car-based and suburbanised than US ones. For a time these might have seemed like cultural lags. Now, however, it appears that in many ways parts of the US are returning to more 'European' modes of life, including railways and urban mass transit systems, delicatessen food (even cheese) and niche markets for cult movies in some of the cities. And if there is a European model, or set of models, of industrial relations, this may well appeal to other regions of the world. Europe also appears 'modern' in relation to the US and many other regions of the world in the extent of its secularisation: whatever the difficulties of measurement in this domain, it is clear that religious belief in Europe has mostly ceased to have the kind of importance for social life as a whole which it has retained elsewhere, even in ostensibly secular states. Scandinavia and East Central Europe have gone furthest in this direction, though France, despite a historically strong Catholic tradition, has also had a strong secular emphasis in education and other matters of state policy (*laicité*) and now displays a relatively high level of disbelief in God.

The resilience of European culture can also of course be seen in a more negative light. How, one might reasonably ask, has a culture made up of constant processes of import and export, in a continent or sub-continent which ruled substantial colonial territories for more than half of the twentieth century, and then received substantial migratory flows from outside Europe in the middle decades of the century, been so relatively untouched by these processes? (Paul Gilroy, whose *Black Atlantic* was a pioneering exploration of a transnational and transcontinental subculture, has also rightly commented on the failure of the dominant culture in England to respond to and value cultural and ethnic difference in a way which is common in North America.[3]) Multiculturalism is a crucially important ideal, but perhaps not yet much of a

---

3. P. Gilroy, *The Black Atlantic. Modernity and Double Consciousness*, Verso 1993.

reality. Nor has the impact on Europe of the technologically more advanced regions elsewhere in the world been as substantial as one might expect. So far, for example, Japanese influences on European culture have not been particularly striking, despite important exceptions in management styles and some areas of design. More generally, the privatism of European ways of life has probably reduced the impact of other cultural influences.

It is not enough, however, to point to distinctivenesses or commonalities in cultural or social forms within Europe, nor even to the frequency and intensity of inter- or transnational interaction. What matters is a more reflexive

'Europe's position as a major cultural producer is an effect of its previous world hegemony'

shaping and incorporation of these common patterns into some sense of identity. A European identity might be seen as taking shape in opposition to, on the one hand, national or subnational identities of a traditional kind and, on the other, alternative supranational identities such as an Anglo-American atlanticist identity, a Francophone (or Hispano- or Lusitano-) or a Mediterranean one. A former supranational candidate, based on the Soviet bloc or 'socialist community of nations' and backed up by the knout of the Brezhnev doctrine, is clearly eliminated. But none of the others seems particularly salient either; the structural relations emerging from the European integration process have probably dealt the *coup de grace* to these anyway somewhat factitious identities. For the core states of the European Union, the euro will probably be a more powerful integrative force than any of these, though even a currency union is not necessarily much more of a *Heimat* than was the German customs union, the *Zollverein*.

On the other hand, and despite the continued massive presence of national infrastructures of all kinds, one should not overlook the growing affinities between inhabitants of the main metropolitan centres in Europe, or within some of the Euroregions. Border regions like Mosel-Rhine, for example, seem to have a real identity, marked in a slightly macabre fashion some years ago when after a bad motorway pile-up casualties were divided between the nearest hospitals, which happened to be in three different countries. But our own regional grouping, East Sussex/Seine-Maritime, has more obstacles to overcome - not least the collapse of the direct ferry service.

Migration, or rather willingness to migrate, is an important index of

Europeanness in the sense relevant here. Clearly Europe scores very low on this dimension compared to the US, where substantial flows from rustbelt to sunbelt and so on have been commonplace. Only in Belgium and Luxemburg does more than 2.5 per cent of the workforce come from another EU member state (*Observer* 7.1.96). Intermarriage in Europe is correspondingly insubstantial - even across the line of the former Berlin Wall, where the East/West German marriage rate is still running at only 3 per cent, as against 16 per cent for marriages between Germans and non-Germans. And despite the rise of the transnational manager, the political classes of Europe remain strikingly national in their composition. The German candidate for French political office Daniel Cohn-Bendit, the Czech former MEP for Italy Jiri Pelikan, or the German-born MP for Birmingham Gisela Stuart remain isolated exceptions. Even in the supranational EU institutions, explicit national quotas exist for appointments, including senior positions such as European commissioner or judge in the European Court. Social movements are somewhat less bound by nation-state boundaries, though for many of course the local nature of their concerns militates against their Europeanisation. There is also no genuinely European newspaper, published in the major languages, and *The European* makes a poor showing compared to the *Herald Tribune* or *Financial Times*.

Before this attempt to look on the bright side of European integration ends up, as in *The Life of Brian*, nailed up or entombed, let me take a step back: *reculer pour mieux sauter*. I take one of the most important elements in recent theorising about and for civil society to have been the realisation that it must be conceived not so much in opposition to as in conjunction with state and other systemic structures, whether or not the term is extended to include them;[4] and it is to these that I now turn rather more explicitly. I am offering therefore one element of a reply to Charles Turner, who has criticised Gellner and Habermas for their undue economism and constitutionalism respectively.[5] There may be good reasons, *pace* Turner, for focusing not just on the associational dimension of civil society but on the

---

4. V. Peres Dias, *The Return of Civil Society*, Harvard University Press 1993; and 'The Public Sphere and a European Civil Society', in J. Alexander (ed), *Real Civil Societies*, Sage 1998.
5. In R. Fine & S. Rai (eds), *Civil Society: Democratic Perspectives*, Cass 1997.

contribution of other political and economic (and even military) structures to the integration process. This is not to justify the dangerous elitism of much European integration politics, with its shameless technocratism and its neglect or patronising of the benighted natives, but it does suggest an open-minded and broad-spectrum approach to Europe-level activities. A European identity may emerge from conflicts in agricultural negotiations as well as from more lofty exercises in pursuit of common values; we should be thinking perhaps in terms of Simmel's model of the integrating effects of conflict rather than a Durkheimian sociology of religion: the management of dissensus, as much as consensus, is an important part of the process of integration. A European identity will also be something highly mediated in a virtual sense, where the real agents are likely to remain predominantly drawn from a limited number of social circles - top managers, experts, political leaders, and the like.

There is of course a further issue here, that of the division between a broadly geographical and cultural *Grosseuropa*, stretching from the Atlantic to at least the Urals and probably the Russian Pacific, and the *Kleineuropa* made up of the member states of the EU at any given point in time. I am implacably opposed to the sloppy equation of 'Europe' with the EU, and the concomitant neglect, for the moment at least, of the 'other Europe'. On the other hand it is clear that the integration process within the EU is the leading edge of European integration conceived more broadly, leaving the non-members as inevitably an outer circle or set of circles.

We may wish, then, for a 'people's Europe' beyond the glass and print temples of the EU institutions, but this will have to develop in some sort of relation with them, rather as communists used to have to define themselves, whether positively or negatively, in relation to the Soviet Union. The slogan 'Yes to Europe, no to Maastricht' was still of course a contribution to the Maastricht debate. This puts the emphasis back again on the EU and its democratic deficit. As Delanty puts it: 'The normative orientation for European identity must be the opening up of the democratic space opened up by European integration ... European identity cannot rest on other criteria than democratic identifications and the ideal of a postnational citizenship.' [6]

---

6. In the Viehoff and Segers collection, p283 - see note 2.

With the collapse of the 'people's democracies', and the eclipse of revolutionary socialism, the liberal democratic state, like capitalism, has no obvious practical alternative. If anything, and despite very important elements of disillusionment or political alienation, it has acquired stronger roots with the democratisation of everyday life: the growing acceptance, exemplified in spheres as diverse as media interviews with politicians and child-rearing practices, that all our decisions and ways of life are in principle open to questioning. They become in Habermas's sense 'post-conventional'. Modernity is, as the German historical sociologist Norbert Elias described it, essentially a 'society of individuals' (see his *The Society of Individuals*, Blackwell 1992); and, as Durkheim recognised, individualism has become something of a substitute for religious belief in modern societies. For example, parents' views on the desirability or otherwise of encouraging independence rather than obedience in their children are an interesting marker of differences across Europe. There are striking differences between the value placed on autonomy in the North and Central region (Austria, West Germany, Netherlands and the Nordic countries) and the emphasis on obedience in the South and West (UK, Ireland, France, Italy, Portugal, Spain).[7] There are similar differences between some parts of Eastern Europe (Hungary, East Germany, and the former Soviet Baltic republics, but also Bulgaria in the south-east) and others (authoritarian Czechoslovakia, Poland, Belorussia and Russia). The domain of working practices and workplace cultures in Europe also displays considerable diversity, with the contrast between corporatist Rhineland capitalism and the neoliberal British version intersecting with that between managerially top-heavy and authoritarian French (and other Latin) enterprises and those in Germany or Scandinavia, where workers have tended to be more skilled, participation more institutionalised and managers less numerous. How far these differences will persist, against a background of globalisation of both economic structures and managerial cultures, is an open question. In both cases, however, it is interesting that the traditional stereotype which contrasts a libertarian or anarchic France with a rigid and authoritarian Germany is contradicted by the evidence.

Individualism may also favour the development of a European identity. The

---

7. G. Therborn, *European Modernity and Beyond. The Trajectory of European Societies 1945-2000*, Sage 1995.

more sovereign and reflexive we are in the construction of our individual identities, the easier it will be for us to foreground a European one. In the political sphere, Habermas has popularised Dolf Sternberger's conception of 'constitutional patriotism' (*Verfassungspatriotismus*) based not on membership of a particular ethnic or national community or Volk but on a rational and defensible identification with a decent constitutional state which may of course be the one whose citizenship one holds as well as the one in which one lives. But as Habermas has also come to stress, if the liberal democratic nation state has few internal enemies, it is increasingly seen as inappropriate to the contemporary reality of global processes and challenges, as well as to the desire of many citizens for more local autonomy. In Daniel Bell's classic phrase, it is 'too small for the big problems of life, and too big for the small problems of life'.[8] In this postnational constellation, as Habermas has called it, the progress of European union, combined as it is with attempts to strengthen regional autonomy under the slogan of subsidiarity, becomes a crucial external determinant of the internal reconfiguration of many European states, notably the UK. Once again, Europe is pioneering a mode of governance - this time transnational rather than national - which gives some practical embodiment to the current extension of democratic thinking into conceptions of cosmopolitan democracy. This development is as important, I believe, as the earlier extension of liberal democracy into social democracy; it coexists uneasily, however, with communitarian thinking, both in social and political philosophy and in the practice of (for example) Clinton and Blair, and to some extent Jospin and Schröder.

The rise of communitarian ideology coexists rather curiously with claims about the end of the social or its replacement by the postsocial (not of course that the protagonists are the same). In a broader prespective, however, an opposition between the large-scale anonymous and formal structures characteristic of modernity and the still-surviving localised (or now sometimes de-localised) communities of co-residents or co-thinkers has been a continuing feature of contemporary Europe. Some thinkers have argued that the rationalisation processes characteristic of modernity have given place to a more disorganised and chaotic postmodern world of disorganised capitalism, franchised

---

8. D. Bell, 'The World and the United States in 2013', *Daedalus*, Vol 116, No 3, 1987, p14.

welfare services and utilities, unstructured belief, chaotic lives made up of juggling a variety of short-term part-time jobs, and so forth. This is I think a mistake, and not just in the sphere of work, where this thesis has been subject to a certain amount of back-pedalling recently. What we find instead, I think, in what some people have called a second modernity, is an accentuation of many of the same processes under conditions where structures have become more complex and virtual, though no less efficacious. Class structures, I suggest, remain crucially important determinants of individuals' life-chances, even if they no longer find a direct embodiment in huge working-class occupational communities or mass organisations. The effects of gender, too, have remained pervasive, even as fewer and fewer occupations are explicitly segregated. In this newly rationalised world, issues of individual identity return in new but still recognisable forms.

We are back, then, with the issue of modernity, and the possibility of decoupling it analytically from the European context in which it initially developed. Asking what is distinctive about European modernity, the French sociologist Henri Mendras (in *L'Europe des Européens*, Gallimard 1997) offers a historical answer which emphasises the long and slow conquest of Europe (by which he means Western Europe) by an ideological model. This model is made up of ideological innovations: the individualist idea of man; the distinction between three types of legitimacy: religious, political and economic; the notion of capital; the combination of science and technology; the power of the majority; the binding force of contract and of the relation of trust which it presupposes; the constitutional state and Roman property law. These are the fundamental elements of western European civilisation, which Mendras argues are unique in the history of civilisation. What is striking in this list, I think, is the way it includes, for good reason, formal-legal relations as well as other beliefs and practices which one might assign to the sphere of civil society.

Modernity is characterised, of course, by a weakening of traditional identities in the anonymity of cities and individual wage-labour. At the same time, we see a desire to categorise and classify, of which Foucault gave the classic examples in his studies of the emergence of the 'mad', 'sick' or 'homosexual' identity. More particularly, the European nation states became concerned to count and measure their populations, and to impose a common national identity at the expense of regional ones. Boundary changes throughout the nineteenth and twentieth centuries, and migration flows within and into Europe, have increasingly subverted the latter process, but many European states continue to try to preserve a traditional line. France, in particular, has resisted expressions of cultural difference in public institutions, in particular the wearing of Islamic headscarves in schools, and is currently opposing a European agreement reached in 1992 to support minority languages.

The important point, however, is that it is increasingly easy for individuals to define themselves in various ways, choosing between a repertoire of identities, and foregrounding one or another according to context. (The frequent adoption in internet chat groups of a fictitious identity or the opposite gender is one of the most recent examples.) Here again we see the inseparable interplay of structural and cultural elements in defining identities. Sexual identity is fairly clear-cut, but its salience in social contexts is highly variable. A homosexual identity may be given a central place by its bearer and his or her associates, or it may be kept in the background by both. Some women may change their names to mark their distinctness from their fathers or parents. There seems however to be an emergent consensus in the incipiently multicultural societies of contemporary Europe that it is up to individuals to define their identities, choosing what weight they wish to attach to each, and that 'outing' and 'othering' are unacceptable. Members of ethnic and religious minorities, in particular, have resisted attempts, no doubt well-meaning, to increase their political representation through the incorporation of traditional elites or 'community leaders'. What strikes me - and here I differ from Therborn - is how relatively hard it has been for Europeans to move to a North American pattern where 'Italian-American', 'African-American' and so on are recognisable identities and where it is understood that the bit before the hyphen will have different degrees of salience for different individuals. There are of course significant fundamentalist counter-movements, which in their turn call forth hysterical responses. More seriously, the fundamentalisms of the 'others' are matched by a 'majority' fundamentalism which refuses ethnic and cultural difference, and in the terms of which a black person, say, can never be 'really' British or French.

The extent to which a European identity has approached the traditional importance of national or regional identities (Scottish, Breton, etc) is again highly variable between and within states. According to the *Eurobarometer* of spring 1999, 'At the EU level, nearly 9 in 10 people feel attached to their country, their town or village and their region. More than half of EU citizens feels attached to Europe'. But in the Netherlands it is only 49 per cent, in Greece 41 per cent and in the UK 37 per cent. More worryingly still, I think it can be argued that, under conditions of advanced modernity, even xenophobia has become reflexive. An awareness of the ways in which misunderstanding and prejudice may be understood forms part of the context underlying them. A newspaper report some years ago that UK students participating in international exchange programmes often returned home more, rather than less hostile to foreigners was neatly illustrated by a cartoon in which one student says to another: 'I hate foreigners because they've turned me into a xenophobe'.

The most intense forms of xenophobia of course remain 'racial', and the term 'European' has been used too often as 'racial' identity for us to be entirely comfortable with it. On the other hand, a focus on a necessarily multicultural Europe held together by cosmopolitan political, social and economic ties may make members of minority ethnic groups feel more comfortable than a more traditional emphasis on notionally homogeneous, if in practice always diverse, 'national' entities. 'British', for example, in formations such as 'Black British' or 'British Asian', has long been offered to ethnic minorities instead of the more marked 'English', 'Welsh' or 'Scottish' - though the growing unacceptability for some of the term 'British' is reflected in, for example, a recent decision not to use it in the Scottish version of the upcoming UK census.

We have learned from thinkers like Elias, Touraine and Giddens to avoid reifiying 'societies', defined by the boundaries of particular states, and it is no less important to avoid reifying 'Europe'. It is clearly an entity with fuzzy edges, and not just because some European states include overseas territories or because Turkey and Russia stretch into Asia. It's also internally fuzzy: the contours of Europe's main traditional divisions are shifting in dramatic ways. It is not just that the old political East/West division has now been replaced by an economic one. The cultural North/South divide within Europe, marked for example by the line between potatoes and pasta, remains important, but is changing in many ways, with the modernisation of (parts of the) southern European societies. It is now for example Italy, rather than the Protestant Northern countries, which (in the absence of adequate child-care provision) apparently puts work before having children. The North-South religious divide remains an important structural principle in Western Europe, as does, further East, that between Orthodox Christianity and Islam. The East-West line also remains crucial, as Germans on both sides (but especially the East) will confirm, and many central Europeans would also continue to stress the distinctiveness of their societies from 'Eastern' Europe as well as from Russia. There are also many similarities between Scandinavia and parts of East Central Europe, despite their diverse political histories for much of the twentieth century.

On the issue of compatibilities and incompatibilities of various structural and cultural forms, Max Weber borrowed from Goethe what remains perhaps the most useful concept for addressing these issues: the chemical concept of elective affinity (*Wahlverwandtschaft*). But if this provides a useful way of thinking about such relations, it does not give us much of an idea about just what fits with what. What is clear, however, is that human societies are much more ingenious in their cultural bricolage or pick-and-mix than we might predict. The current attention to conceptions of hybridity is helpful here, though even this term risks implying a certain reification of the initial entities between which hybridising occurs. It seems fair to expect, however, that despite the Americanising pull of the mass media, reflecting and reinforcing the appeal of North America and to some extent Australia to many young Europeans, Europe will remain culturally distinct from other world regions, with local differences persisting against a background of common European and global systems. The washing powder, for example, may have instructions in many languages and contact addresses in half a dozen countries, but the fine detail of domestic work will continue to display interesting differences across the continent. The interrelations between post-conventional post-national identities, in competition with more atavistic traditional national identities, and a European identity itself ambivalent in relation to this antithesis, will form the broader social and cultural background to the ups and downs of the political and economic project of European integration in the early twenty-first century.

I am grateful to Gerard Delanty, Jenneth Parker and Larry Ray for comments on this essay; also to Andreas Hess and other participants in the 'Uncivil Dimensions of Civil Society' conference.

Misunderstandings and misleading stereotypes

A Western feminist goes East

Claire Wallace

Claire Wallace *reflects on what feminists in Eastern and Western Europe can learn from each other, and on the prospect facing women in the former communist countries.*

When in 1991 I first arrived in Prague to teach a group of students gathered together from all over the former Soviet block for a course in 'Society and Politics', I knew that their experiences would be different to mine. I wanted to understand their perspectives as much as promulgate my own. I arrived fresh from organising Women's Studies courses in England, where the lecture theatres were overflowing with students wanting to learn this subject, and where such courses always attracted applicants - indeed they were used as a 'selling point' for the University. I arrived from a situation where feminist ideas had been excitedly discussed amongst academic women who willingly gave their own time to found study groups and develop courses. I arrived from a situation where my own intellectual and emotional development as a student had been shaped by critical theories which seemed to offer not only radical insights into the nature of contemporary capitalist society but to give shape to vague feelings of discontent with contemporary gender relations: in other words, to offer not just a way of discussing society but also changing it self-consciously for the better. Those theories were feminist ones. I arrived from an intellectual tradition (sociology) which had to a great extent been shaped by feminism over the previous twenty years: for me feminism had provided most of the original and exciting intellectual ideas since my undergraduate days, and had suggested new ways of understanding my discipline. I had myself written a number of books and articles to analyse this process.

However, I found the reception of these ideas very different in post-communist Eastern Europe. Feminist ideas were greeted with lack of interest or even downright hostility. When I brought up the subject it certainly inspired students - it inspired them to write essays on why feminism is irrelevant in Eastern Europe. This was not simply my experience. A male lecturer had an even more hostile response when he suggested a course on 'Gender, Sexuality and Sexual Politics' (ideas at the forefront of much sociological debate at that moment). He was told by one of the students (a woman), 'We thought you were a *serious* scholar and now you do this'. Another (a man) informed him 'I would like to kill you'. Seldom do courses inspire such passionate resentment.

I soon learned not to use the word 'feminism' and to leave that part of my identity behind - or at any rate less forefronted. Over the past four years I have been able to reflect further on some of these ideas, with the advantage of being able to talk with a range of women and men from the region who are interested in gender issues. I have found that many of my ideas were irrelevant or offensive to such people, and this has helped me to reconsider my own ideas about the direction of feminist thought and the universal appropriateness of feminist concepts which were developed in a western academic context. In arguing with students and colleagues I have become critical of some aspects of the feminist movement as it applies to post-communist experience; but this has also helped me to understand where and in what ways an appreciation of gender is needed. In trying to listen to and understand the perspectives being offered to me, I was able to reflect upon and recast some of my own ideas. I discovered that although men and women in both halves of Europe were often concerned about the same issues, they were talking about them in different ways: they were in the same seminar but talking past each other, with mutual misunderstandings being created.

In this article I want to consider the relevance of a gender perspective to post-communist transition and the theories which are being developed in this context. Then I will turn to some misunderstandings of feminist ideas in a post-communist context: work, family, political participation and reproductive rights. These are areas where feminist discourse has developed some of its most important insights but where women from the different ideological divides are most likely to be talking past each other.

However, firstly it is important to make a more general point about the emerging gender discourse in Central and Eastern Europe. Much of the discussion has taken place in the period since the iron curtain was stripped away - a time when western feminist ideas had already reached a mature stage of intellectual development. The context for debate was thus very different.

W omen in Western Europe and the USA who were developing feminist ideas were often also veterans of struggles for better rights and conditions for women - on issues such as abortion, childcare, lesbian rights, equal opportunities and so on. Such hard-won victories had often leant a militant edge to their rhetoric. Their voice was often one of sarcasm and outrage. This relationship between theories and action was often a problematic one, as any one who has taught on a women's studies course or attended a conference can attest. It is evident that feminist ideas (which have problematised gender relations) are not just theories but are related to a particular political perspective and a political movement, however diffuse that might be. They are not just dispassionate theories but ones which imply a programme of social action and which demand that the person who espouses them takes sides. This partisan perspective is anathema to many social scientists and intellectuals in East and Central Europe because they value the scientific objectivity of their disciplines after decades of political distortion. For them it is an essential part of their identity and their purpose in life to keep 'science' separate from politics.

The feminist movement in the West had blossomed in a number of different forms and colours, giving a multiplicity of ideas and perspectives in a range of different disciplines (both new and old) which cross-fertilised each other: literature influenced sociology and sociology influenced history. Gay studies influenced black studies and black studies influenced women's studies and so on ...This in turn produced a proliferation of literature in the form of books, novels, journals, articles and so on. Women's studies and feminism had established a 'niche' in universities, in publishing and amongst funding organisations.

In the initial phases of post-communist transition this put western intellectuals in a more powerful position. They were able to fund conferences and scholarships and were able to set the intellectual agenda according to their own concerns. Here was the opportunity to 'help' their Eastern European 'sisters' just struggling to emerge from authoritarian societies. This was a cause that could be championed, an opportunity to show the way and to pass on the lessons which they had learned, to set some good examples, to demonstrate their achievements, of what could be done 'in the west'. Although people set out on this project with the best possible intentions, from the other side it could be seen as at best patronage, at worst imperialism. This resource imbalance was also reflected in an imbalance of numbers. The far-reaching influence of feminism in some intellectual circles in western Europe was counteracted by the lack of interest in feminism by the majority of eastern European intellectuals; and the very few who were interested were compelled to address the issues which western feminists set them. As one Czech woman put it, they felt like zoo animals being displayed at conferences and meetings.[1] But they also felt that nobody really listened to their ideas because these ideas did not fit easily within western feminist perspectives - and even challenged western feminist perspectives. This is not to say that Eastern European women did not have strong views on gender: on the contrary. But these views often emphasised maternity, the possibility of a 'feminine' alternative, the rejection of conventional politics and work roles - things which did not fit very comfortably with western feminists who had been struggling for many years to oppose these things or to fight for political representation. Therefore it was difficult for post-communist intellectuals to make their voices heard and even more difficult for western women to listen to them. They were coming from a different situation, a different set of experiences, and needed to define their position in new ways.

This initial phase has now passed, and there is now a developing discourse of post-communist intellectuals on the subject of gender. In many ways this discourse challenges the assumptions of western feminism. (The nearest parallel

---

1. *Bodies of Bread and Butter*, edited by S. Trnka, and L. Busheikin, and published by the Prague Gender Studies Centre in 1993, explores many of these issues.

to this is probably the critical work by black women who have challenged the implicit assumptions about masculinity and femininity which were embedded in feminist ideas developed mainly from a white perspective.) East European women, armed with their experiences both under communism and in newly emerging market societies, are finding that many of the universalising assumptions about gender held within western feminism apply only to those contexts in which they originated. The experience of post-communist women speaks differently, and their intellectual training predisposes them to different styles of explanation.

The lack of a gender perspective in theories of post-communist transition

I have often been informed that there are more important and urgent things to think about than gender in the post-communist world - for example political and economic transformation. Gender relations are a trivial distraction from these important concerns and reflect the fact that some western scholars have nothing better to do in their societies, I am told. It is certainly true that Eastern Europe faces very dire problems of impending or existing war, ethnic tension, rapid privatisation, physical survival and so on. However, to assume that gender is irrelevant to these issues is erroneous. The main problem is a lack of a critical gender perspective in most theories of communist transition - which often reflect the main preoccupations in those societies.

For example, nationalism has been one of the key issues in the emergence from communism. And the resurgence of nationalism can be understood as a way of reforging patriarchal relations, with male and female roles being inscribed into new forms of defence of the nation state, and of aggression against others. The very small number of people who have tried to bring a gender perspective to bear on this issue have indicated that this redefinition of nationalism involves the redefinition of male roles in terms of warriors and aggressors, defenders of the ethnos. The female duty is to bear the next generation of cultural defenders. This reflects a tendency to reinforce 'traditional' gender roles in the aftermath of the imposed ideology of communist equality. Nowhere is this more obvious than in the mass rapes in Yugoslavia. Although rape is always a consequence of warfare (something which feminists have brought to popular attention) - as a way in which one aggressing group can attack another

- gender relations are at the heart of such acts of warfare, and provide powerful propaganda to inspire men to further fighting if they feel they are to lose patriarchal control over 'their' women. This is warfare over the territory of women's bodies as much as physical territory.

However, rape as an instrument of humiliation and violation of a person's integrity is not used solely against women. Reports from refugees indicated that a significant number of men were also being raped in the most recent Balkan war. The importance of a new swaggering machismo, drawing upon a range of popular cultural symbols, including rambo-style headbands, and casually displayed military hardware such as guns, knives and so on, is frequently reported by journalists. It creates a new violent aesthetic, a popular cultural fashion of warfare. The symbolism which serves to reinforce male bonding in gangs is particularly salient in situations where other forms of social order have broken down. The new, primitive masculinity is an essential corollary of the situation being created. The analysis of forms of masculinisation which accompany the militarisation of societies is little explored, but this is an important issue which can bring useful insights into other areas, for example industrial relations. This aspect of gender relations, which is an integral part of warfare, seldom engages the attention of western feminist writers, who in the main consider war to be beyond their interests - especially as war so close to home is an unfamiliar experience for the current generation of European intellectuals, and one they might prefer to forget.

The debate about civil society has gained new ground with regard to the transition from communism. However, whilst the relationship between civil society and family life is sometimes discussed, it is seldom more than a passing reference. In general the participation of women in civil society, and the way in which this may reconstruct gender roles, is hardly mentioned in the prodigious literature on the subject. One aspect of this discussion is the role of non-governmental organisations, traditionally an area where women's participation has been crucial, and which has been seen as a women's sphere. However, the gendered nature of this kind of non-state civil participation is never discussed.

Discussion of the informal economy has been very important in understanding the transformations in Eastern and Central Europe. The multiple economic roles which people adopt both inside and outside the official economy, along with self-help and household production, which helped households to survive economic crisis both before the changes and in the current period, have been crucial. However, the role which women play in this kind of domestic production - and the role which their networks and activities play in the informal procurement and exchange of goods - is not discussed. This particular form of articulation between the household and economic life is clearly dependent upon gender roles which are developed within the household, but there is almost no discussion of this in the theories which have been developed to account for this aspect of social life - even though it was often feminists who drew attention to the importance of non-waged work in developed capitalist societies.

Other theories about democratisation seldom discuss the differential impact which it has had on gender roles, and upon issues to do with gender. Women's voting is seldom more than a variable. Discussions of privatisation, of informal economic activity or of social policy reform seldom take a gendered perspective, even though they all have important implications for gender roles; and in the discussions about migration the exploitation of women, both sexually and economically - which is routine and widespread - is almost never mentioned.

I could elaborate many more examples, but I think those mentioned so far are sufficient to illustrate the 'gender blind' character of most of the dominant theories of transition in post-communist societies. Feminist debates have been carried out in a separate corner, reinforcing the impression that feminism is irrelevant to the main issues arising from current social transformations.

It could be said therefore that feminist ideas have failed to address the main issues and debates concerning post-communist transformation; but this is not because they are irrelevant - they have simply not been elaborated in this direction. Rather, feminist debates and theories have developed their own dynamic, which often seems rather esoteric and frivolous to people concerned with the radical reconstruction of their society. The current concerns with sexuality, with consumer society or with post-modernism, seem like luxuries available only in an affluent society; they are not seen as addressing fundamental social concerns. The postmodernist deconstruction of gender categories was developing its arguments at a time when such concepts were unlikely to hold much appeal for societies in the process of re-shaping gender roles; and such deconstruction is unhelpful in a context where first what is needed is a re-evaluation of the position of women. Getting rid of the category of 'woman' altogether (as some contemporary feminist theory tends to do) could become a convenient way for gender issues to be altogether left out from the debates on transition. Again, this misunderstanding is perhaps because of the lack of an elaboration of these ideas in such a way as to be relevant to the experiences of women and men in these new social contexts. Issues of differentiation and identity are actually crucial to an understanding of social transformation, and here ideas developed within gender studies have much to offer. But they need to be translated and apprehended.

Women in Eastern Europe are often very self-critical about what they perceive as their own relatively impoverished position in relation to the rich development of gender studies in the west. Jirina Siklova, one of the main feminist spokeswomen in the region, for example, pleads that they need time to develop their own perspective. And Jirina Smejklova-Strickland hypothesises that the deconstruction of sexual difference must begin with the female subject first finding a voice with which to commence the task of deconstruction - and that this hasn't happened yet (see *Bodies of Bread and Butter*). This represents a kind of 'cultural cringe', an apology for not being as well prepared as western feminists on their own ground. However, I think that there are also ways in which women in Eastern Europe can contribute to an auto-critique within feminism generally, and I shall illustrate this by describing various misunderstandings that have arisen, and looking at important debates where women from across the ideological divide are simply talking past each other.

Misunderstanding number 1: gender and work

The experiences of Eastern European women, who have seen their lives as full-time workers, certainly puts them in a different position to many western women. Western feminism derived originally from the struggles of middle-class women for access to Higher Education and employment, in a situation where confinement to the home represented an exclusion from the most valued arenas of public life. This experience is clearly not one which is common to Eastern European women, and they are therefore beginning from a different perspective. However, under the communist system gender issues were far from being 'solved', and 'liberation through participation in production' was not in fact liberation, whilst other more conservative models of gender ideology continued to pervade communist societies. The domestic division of labour and the 'naturalistic' nature of gender roles were never challenged, resulting in a 'double burden' for women both inside and outside of the workplace. These naturalistic roles for women were embedded in the previous communist order but are also very evident in contemporary discussions of women's position: that women are responsible for children and household management is never questioned.

Women in the region can argue that they experienced 'liberation' through productive employment as compulsory labour power stoking engines of the great socialist transformation, and that now they are disillusioned with it. Being forced to work 'like a man' did not make them into men but imposed additional pressures. Although there were advantages for women in terms of access to Higher Education and employment - and this remains a legacy from the previous system - their struggle lies in trying to reconcile conflicting demands in a context where there is no part-time work, but there is a very strong ideology of the family. Liberation is seen as lying in an increasing diversity of choices of life-style and a more satisfactory integration of motherhood and work.

This problematic was also recognised by some feminists in the 1980s in western Europe, who criticised the dominant, androcentric model of a career-driven biography as the ultimately fulfilling goal. But in what some have termed a 'post-feminist' western world - that is, one where the right of women to have the same rights as men is taken for granted and where women can confidently behave in the same way as men - the new generation of women are striving to seize men's privileges. They define their sexuality in their own terms and they behave just as they want. In their exhilaration at finding themselves in higher positions in the work hierarchy, western women have adopted men's values for their own, along with their salaries and their company cars. Eastern European women can tell them that this is not the road to liberation - and they do not fling themselves into this struggle with the same vigour. However, this is not to say that materialism has no purchase. On the contrary, the glittering symbols of market success seem ever more alluring in societies where equality of low salaries was formerly maintained as an economic principle.

However, the shift to a market society in the East has brought about a masculinisation of high income, high achievement jobs. Market relations offer new roles for men. As one of my respondents in Poland told me: men go out and 'hunt' for money. They can compensate for the emasculated role which they suffered under communism by enjoying a more aggressive and macho role as huntsmen in the market. These new roles for men mean more backseat roles for women. They are accompanied by marketing and advertising which appeals to men as managers, movers and shakers in the new capitalist world (one example of this was a poster of a woman's bottom, which was aimed at managers to encourage them to advertise). The gaze was male rather than female: are there no female managers any more? Women are portrayed as secretaries, assistants and people delighted with the purchase of office equipment, clothes or household goods. In the new indigenous advertising campaigns

> 'men compensate for their former emasculated role by becoming macho huntsmen in the market'

scantily dressed women are required to sell anything from beer to bingo. The new advertising is therefore stridently sexist and strongly reinforces the role of the man as making significant decisions in society. The gendering of roles in this process is a part of marketisation, and is not irrelevant to it, as new sets of social relations are being forged and a climate created for the acceptance of new roles.

Gender is a source of increasing social differentiation. Although in communist societies women traditionally earned less than men, and were rarely represented amongst the senior managers or politicians, the communist ideology of equality at least provided some token representation and opportunities - for example to return to jobs after quite lengthy child care leave. This has now been swept aside. In the new emerging inequalities women as single parents have become some of the poorest members of society (this is consistent with most western countries), as have elderly people (more often women). Women are amongst those most likely to be unemployed - for example in the Russian Federation in 1992 women constituted 52 per cent of the workforce but 71 per cent of the unemployed - and they find themselves no longer able to return to their jobs after having children. The absence of effective legislation against discrimination (and the lack of interest in passing any) means that they can be openly discriminated against to an extent which would not be allowed in most western countries: employers in Poland, for example, have been able to compel women to sign documents that they will not get pregnant if they get the job. Jobs can be advertised throughout Eastern and Central Europe with quite sexist specifications (this is not illegal); and sexual harassment is a routine aspect of many kinds of employment. Increasingly it is women, especially those with domestic responsibility, who are losing out in the labour market.

However, any critique of such practices needs also to take into account the excitement that exists about the possibility of new gender roles and relations. The post-communist world offers more of a variety of possibilities which women are able to take advantage of. The possibility for women and men to choose such roles rather than have them forced upon them should be explored, rather than a one-sided and simplistic view of what is right or wrong.

Misunderstanding number 2: the family

In communist and post-communist countries the family has been of central importance to economic survival as well as affective identity. In a situation where childbearing was nearly universal maternity was very highly valued as an element of women's existence. In the formal hierarchy of values out in the public world, women's roles were not so strong (they were under-represented on Central Committees and so on), but these relations were not considered so important. In the informal world of social relations the family and family networks held a prominent place, and here women's participation had far greater value. The family really was the haven in a corrupt and heartless world, representing one of the few sources of meaningful relationships. Peggy Watson, in exploring this phenomenon, argues that with post-communism the relationship between public and private spheres is changing, and increasing gender inequalities are going unremarked.[2] Previously the private sphere was a source of power and importance, so that women who had a prominent position within it were also in a powerful position within the informal hierarchy of values.

For this reason people of Eastern and Central Europe are reluctant to countenance a stringent critique of family relations, which has been one of the contributions made by feminism. In discussions in seminars about sexual or violent family abuse, many students are surprised that this sort of thing is so common in western countries. They assure me that it does not take place in their own countries, or at least not to the same extent. This idea that pathologies in family and gender relations somehow end at the boundary of the former iron curtain, and the reluctance to explore the darker side of family life, can to some extent be explained by the rather sacred role that family relations

---

2. P. Watson, 'Eastern Europe's Silent Revolution: Gender', *Sociology* 27 3 1993.

had in a society where other relations were subject to suspicion and silence.

Maternity was reinforced in a situation where nearly everybody got married and had children. Maternity in particular was a very meaningful and important aspect of a woman's identity. Divorce was also high, and nearly all children in single-parent families were raised by women. Women therefore raised children but also undertook extensive domestic labour, and it was women's networks, especially their own mothers', which made much social life possible. Grandmothers raised children in order to help working mothers and it was this female line which remained stable even when divorce severed affinal links. In this context a number of commentators in significant positions, from Gorbachev in Russia to Emilia Kovacova in Slovakia (the wife of President Michal Kovac), were able to state that the removal of state coercion and the liberalisation of society would allow women to 'go back' to their primordial roles in the family.

> In our society the woman plays two roles; she is mother and at the same time she is the working person-breadwinner. If the couple has better income and sufficient family allowances, I believe that it would not be necessary for the women to work and they could devote their time to their primary vocation - to childrearing. Only this can guarantee the happy future for our country and for the following generations.[3]

This assumes that there are such primordial roles - though as I shall demonstrate later, gender differed very markedly through the region.

With the changes wrought by the introduction of market relations, the informal, family sphere becomes down-graded in importance in relation to the public sphere. As men can go and perform and achieve in the public sphere, the family becomes not such an important source of identity and self-esteem. When people can say whatever they like publicly, the family is not so important as the repository of authentic relations. However, as the family is left behind in the re-valuation of the public sphere, so women - central to the family - are left behind with it. They have lost out not only in the formal sphere of relations, as

---

3. Emilia Kovacova, interviewed in *Smena* 21.7. 1994, translated and cited by Ivan Chorvat in his unpublished thesis, 'Some Historical, Political and Ideological Aspects of Family Life: the impact of industrialization, totalitarianism and feminism on the family', Central European University, Department of Sociology, Prague 1994.

their representation disappears in politics and public life, but also in the informal sphere as it becomes less important. The masculinisation of public life either through 'hunting' in the market place or competitive politics means that women find it harder and harder to compete - especially as their values do not always incline them in this direction.

Western feminists are seen as somehow out to attack and undermine the family. Feminism is associated with women who neglect their children for their own selfish interests. As one student put it: they do not think who will care for family members if they achieve their liberation. The emancipation of women is seen as being at the expense of children. This is rather similar to the critique advanced by Charles Murray, George Gilder and other 'backlash' spokesmen against feminism in the US. And this perhaps accounts for the popularity of some of these authors in East and Central Europe - although so far the connection has not been made between women's liberation and single parent families, and hence crime and rising welfare expenditure. The rising rates of divorce, single parenthood and other forms of 'postmodern' family forms has been a striking feature of western societies and this trend is also being reflected in Eastern European societies. It reflects a general trend towards 'individualisation' and changing life-styles, rather than being anything for which feminism can be blamed. We might counter: why should it be mainly women who are responsible for other family members?

Women are tired. Many female students in both discussions and essays mentioned that women feel overburdened by their multiple roles in communist and also in post-communist societies. As full-time workers, the main carers in the family, and as people having to carry out these tasks without the aid of consumer-durable and labour-saving devices, as well as having to queue and to struggle for the means of subsistence (this is still the case in many post-Soviet countries), they would like to put down some of these burdens. For women in East-Central Europe housework has been far more onerous than for women in the west. They had to produce many basic commodities by growing food and preserving or pickling it; almost no services are commodified so that even now they must clean windows, iron clothes and so on - services which in many western countries are commodified, on the formal or informal market. The enormous range of domestic tasks undertaken even by female entrepreneurs is documented by

Stastna, and always astonishes the audiences to which she presents this information.[4] Women cope with this by mobilising kin networks, especially their mothers, which reinforces links across generations and between family members. For many women the idea of becoming a full-time housewife seems rather attractive, and the new images of glamour and personal attractiveness associated with some of these roles may seem very appealing to women worn out by production and reproduction. The new image of women able to adorn themselves and dress up in scanty clothes can seem at first sight preferable to the dour, serious and unadorned images of women which were presented previously. There is an impulse to celebrate difference rather than homogeneity between the sexes.

Any discussion of the role of women in Eastern and Central Europe must therefore take into account their roles as mothers and more generally within the family, which has a greater meaning and importance than in many countries from which western feminists originate.

Misunderstanding number 3: political representation

In the west we often measure women's success in society in terms of their representation in public office, especially parliament. In Eastern Europe, although women did not hold an equal share of the highest offices, a 'quota' system operating in many countries served to ensure that they were better represented than in most western countries. However, this political participation was obligatory, and was not the outcome of struggles by women for representation. Years of this kind of token representation, and weariness with having to wave the flag at the right moment on official occasions, has bred a cynicism about this kind of public participation. As Hana Havelkova has pointed out in a number of articles, women did not strive for public office, because these positions were not valued by most people.[5] Women were happy to sidestep such obligations in favour of the informal and more meaningful networks of family and friendship. The quota system reinforced an inferiority complex rather than offering the opportunity for advancement. In the course of the transformation period, women

---

4. J. Stastna, 'Women Entrepreneurs in the Czech Republic', unpublished research, Central European University, Prague 1994.
5. H. Havelkova, 'Some Pre-Feminist Thoughts', in N. Funk and M. Muller (eds), *Feminism and Post-Communism*, Routledge 1993.

happily stepped down from such onerous burdens, but in the process they have often been left out, now that the public sphere is more important in generating key policies and decisions.

Where women have been publicly active it is often through their roles as mothers. Thus a movement called 'Prague Mothers against Pollution' explicitly eschews any feminist connections and campaigns instead for issues which affect their children. The emphasis is on women's maternal responsibilities, and their political representation as mothers, which then leads them to make other kinds of protest for a better world for their children. This position is rather difficult for women coming from a western feminist perspective to grasp. Although women's protest using female symbols has been one aspect of the new social movements emerging in the West in recent decades (as the protests around Greenham Common made clear), this protest as mothers is a new experience. Political gestures which are outside mainstream politics have been an important element of the women's movement, but they have never been made in quite the same way as the 'Prague Mothers' protest.

The experiences of women in post-communist countries can teach us that political representation is not the only, or even perhaps the most important, form of power. It can also be form of alienation.

Misunderstanding number 4: reproductive rights

One of the main campaigning issues of feminism has been in the sphere of reproductive rights. From marches to defend the right to abortion to critiques of the new reproductive technologies, feminists have always argued for the right for women to control their own bodies and their own fertility.

In Eastern and Central Europe this is even more of a salient issue, since contraceptives have not been widely available until recently (and are still not widely available in many areas), and where abortion has been used as a means of controlling fertility, especially after the first or second childbirth. However, in some contexts abortion was seen as an aspect of state or even imperial control. For example in Lithuania it has been argued that this was introduced by the Russians as a way of keeping down the Lithuanian population. Abortion methods were damaging to health, but this was not perceived to be an area of interest for feminists. Only in Poland, where access to abortion was severely restricted by the post-communist governments, and where contraception also came under critical fire from the church, was there some mobilisation of public opinion about reproductive rights (although it was not sufficient to prevent some of the most draconian anti-abortion legislation in Europe being passed). Although women are the most religious sex in Poland and are most likely to go church, they may also disagree with the church on this and other issues.

The manipulation of reproduction as an instrument of state policy has crucial implications for women's ability to lead independent lives based upon a choice of life-style, but so far, despite the considerable suffering of Eastern and Central European women, this has failed to become an issue for feminists.

In the post-communist world, the control of fertility is not necessarily seen as a positive aspect of women's liberation, especially where previously existing methods of control were painful and horrible, and were carried out because of a state policy to maximise women's productive potential. The choice of available and unharmful forms of birth control must be an essential element of women's right to self-determination, but this is not seen as a priority issue.

The misunderstandings I have outlined here are not helped by the fact that those in East and West Europe often hold unhelpful stereo-types of each other, through which lens images and ideas are distorted. Here I shall explore two such stereotypes: 'western feminists' and 'East European women'.

Misleading stereotypes number 1: 'Western feminists'

Western feminists are often jeered at in the popular press, even by important and otherwise enlightened figures such as Vaclav Havel. The image is that these are screeching harridans with psychological problems, they are extremely unattractive, they are probably lesbian and they are unhappy in their private lives. At the very least they have difficulty attracting a man. Nobody could possibly want to be such a person, it is assumed.

Many people believe that gender equality was already achieved under socialism. Unlike in the west, women went to work, they competed with men, and the problems of gender inequality have been solved. This was repeated to me again and again in interviews conducted in Poland. To quote one of the respondents, a male student in his early twenties:

> I think there is no problem with the rights of men and women. I don't think
> that there is any special discrimination of women in Poland and in my
> personal opinion, there shouldn't be ... So I don't know why such a topic
> came into being, because I don't think it is a real problem. Maybe it is some
> sort of female complex to raise such an issue?

This reflects the idea projected under communism that gender relations were no longer a 'problem', and that it is somehow artificial to create this problem. The assumption is that because this problem was 'solved' by communism it is also not a problem under post-communism, despite increasing evidence of inequality between the sexes.

Many young women also expressed similar opinions, although in a survey of 1913 young people between the ages of 18 and 24 carried out in Poland in 1993 young women were significantly more likely to support a more equitable division of labour in the home, and the possibility of women getting better jobs in the labour market, than were young men.[6] Although they would strongly support the idea of women's right to self-determination, to a negotiated division of labour, and to work in the labour market, they would never associate those things with some ghastly feminist.

There is a very monolithical view of feminism, whereas in fact there are very different kinds of feminists with many different and often incompatible viewpoints. Some feminists have a more 'conservative' orientation, in trying to recognise or even celebrate women's roles within reproduction as carers and nurturers. Others have rejected this view and strive instead for more equal recognition in public life. The deep divisions between the radical and separatist feminists, as compared with more liberal ones, is only one example of the many differences of opinion existing within the feminist movement. In fact it is almost impossible to describe it as 'a' movement any more. The only thing uniting feminists is a questioning approach to gender: but in seeing gender as a problem, a whole range of answers or solutions can arise.

Whilst in the US a regard for women's issues can take a number of forms, from reform of the law to the preservation of family life, in Europe

---

6. C. Wallace, 'Polish young women at the crossroads', working paper, Central European University 1995.

much feminist rhetoric and perspective arose out of the socialist movement, particularly in the 1970s. This means that many of the metaphors and ideas were translated from socialism into feminism, even for those feminists who rejected socialist solutions to social problems. Hence, ideas such as 'sisterhood is global' or the idea that women represented an 'oppressed group' or that there was an inevitable 'struggle' of the sexes were outcomes of this alliance of socialism or Marxism and feminism. However, such metaphors and concepts have very negative connotations for women in Eastern and Central Europe. The stridently militant use of expressions and campaigns which this encouraged reminded women who had grown up under really existing socialism of the tired slogans of their former regimes, which were used only as labels to mask a different reality. Furthermore, people who had been obliged to participate with revolutionary fervour in the great socialist experiment, through demonstrating or mouthing the appropriate choice of words - forms of participation for which there was little enthusiasm by the 1980s - saw in many feminist expressions a similar kind of rhetoric

> The hatred, the militantly ideological manifestations of some feminists, and the ideological character of feminist trends, make us feel the same nausea which in the past we experienced with references to the 'class struggle' (J. Siklova, in *Bodies of Bread and Butter*).

Expressions which to western feminists seemed strong and thrilling provoked only nausea in those who had been obliged to live under them.

Trying to understand this has made me wince at some of these expressions which I have used myself. Things which can seem appropriate in opposition may be inappropriate as a part of a dominant ideology. Furthermore, they have made me question my own assumptions as to what such over-generalised categories may mean. The rather simplifying vocabulary indicating a combative war of the sexes does not do justice to the complexity of subtle differences, alliances and oppositions implied in contemporary gender roles. Reducing the world to a Manichean cosmic conflict is neither theoretically nor empirically helpful, and it certainly alienates women in East and Central Europe whose experience it does not accurately represent.

Misleading stereotypes number 2: 'East European women'

However, just as it is dangerous to generalise about 'western feminism' as though it was a unified set of ideas and politics, so it is dangerous to generalise about 'Eastern and Central European women'. The differences between these countries, which were hitherto more submerged, are starting to surface and to increase, as countries move at different speeds of economic development.

In a fascinating essay about the experiences of Russian women, Olga Isupova argues that pre-revolutionary Russian peasant society imposed very hard roles upon women.[7] They worked in the fields and did much productive work as well as having primary responsibility for the home. This very active role for women is poles apart from that of the cloistered bourgeois women who became the original objects of western feminist critical scrutiny. The lack of a bourgeoisie in Russia, and its destruction after the revolution, meant that their roles were not generalised in this region. After the revolution, the enforced participation of women in full-time productive work was an extension of the roles they had performed previously, although now they were more likely to work in factories rather than in fields. Furthermore, the enormous slaughter of Russian men in the revolution, the civil war and the Second World War, meant that many Russian women were left performing all the roles in Russian society as well as doing all the work. Therefore 'socialist ideals' of equality were built upon traditional roles and de facto necessity.

In other areas of the former communist block, such as the Czech Republic, which had been a more bourgeois society, the enforced productive role of women was more of a violation of what had taken place previously (although in this country there was a very well-developed bourgeois feminist movement before the Nazi invasion, which also formed a part of the national liberation struggle at the end of the nineteenth century). In countries such as Hungary or Bulgaria communism brought women out of the fields and cottages and into the factories and cities - into public life. Throughout the region the communist expansion of education benefited women in particular, who outnumber men in many branches of Higher Education, creating a generation of women with high expectations. The experience of Rumanian women with the draconian pro-natalist policy of

---

7. O. Isupova, 'Symbolic Representations about Gender Roles in Contemporary Russian Society', unpublished MA dissertation, Central European University, Prague 1994.

Ceauceauscu did not have parallels elsewhere; nor do the current experiences of Polish women in a country where the Catholic Church's involvement in politics has led to anti-abortion and anti-contraceptive legislation. On the other hand, it was in that country that a woman Prime Minister proved one of the most effective leaders. In Eastern Germany, where the issue has probably been most extensively debated, there was another experience: under communism generous social policies for family support enabled women to become fairly independent economically, and this encouraged a higher rate of single parenthood than in other countries. However, their absorption by Western Germany has meant the removal of such benefits and sudden imposition of far more conservative gender policies.

As well as these differences between countries, there are now increasingly acknowledged differences within countries, with different ethnic minorities holding different places in the labour market and having different patterns of family reproduction and family relations. Differences for example between Turks and Bulgarians in Bulgaria, or between Russians and others in Central Asian countries, are significant.

Women from different countries have experienced different kinds of gender oppression and gender roles. We should therefore be careful about generalising about 'women' from the region as though they were all the same.

Conclusions

In this essay I have attempted to explore some of the misunderstandings and misleading stereotypes which have clouded communication between intellectuals interested in gender issues in East and West Europe. I have tried to indicate ways in which it is necessary to understand what people in the region are telling us, because they can offer important insights into contemporary post-communist, post-material, post-modern (or however you characterise it) society. They can also suggest limitations and 'blind spots' in contemporary feminist theories. They can suggest new ways forward based upon different experiences and different philosophical perspectives.

The disintegration of the iron curtain has thrown a number of post-war assumptions as well as post-war social and political theories into disarray. The study of societies in the throes of radical transformation offers new insights into the contemporary social world. The disappearance of old dichotomies such as 'East' and 'West', 'Left' and 'Right', 'Communist' and 'Capitalist' as well as - maybe - 'male' and 'female' opens the space for new ways of characterising the social world.

Women in post-communist East and Central Europe are struggling to understand such changes and to come to terms with their own experiences. In the case of the leading intellectuals, their own biographies have spanned both the communist system and the post-communist one, so that this means a search for a new understanding of their own lives as well as their intellectual projects. This soul-searching is evident in their efforts to understand their position as women in the changes. However, a new generation of young women are now entering intellectual life for whom the memory of the communist system is more remote, and who want to forge a new set of relationships in the contemporary world. These young women are the best educated generation to emerge so far from this part of Europe, and have watched their mothers performing all the productive and reproductive roles which were necessary to make social life possible. They are now faced with multiple gender identities and many perspectives through which to understand them. They are enjoying the excitement and exhilaration of having a range of choices none of which are pre-determined. It is these young women who are unlikely either to 'go back to the home' and fulfil the classic model of the nuclear family, or to uncritically accept some model of primordial roles, even where they live in societies which are militarising and nationalising. They will offer interpretations filtered through a new set of intellectual and material experiences.

Some important initiatives have already taken place. Various 'networking' schemes are very active in bringing together those who are interested in these issues, but may be scattered around many different countries and institutions. Other schemes, such as that which founded the Prague Gender Studies Centre, have taken the form of raising money and simply giving it to women in the region to develop in their own way. Such initiatives are all examples of positive ways forward, and ways in which men and women interested in these issues can work together. However, they have tended to follow a West-East axis, and there is still some scope for women from different Eastern European countries to develop their own networks and channels of communication.

Furthermore, the dialogue continues ... I hope that this will be one contribution.

I would like to acknowledge the contributions of Larissa Flint, Laura Busheikin, and all the others at the Prague Gender Studies Centre, as well as those of Lucie Cviklova, Ivan Chorvat, Olga Isupova, Jaroslava Stastna, Julie Beck, Peter Lentini and Troy McGrath at the Central European University.

Afterword

I wrote this article as I was leaving Prague in 1994, after working for four years at the Central European University there. At the time I was filled with idealism about the possibility of new intellectual and social movements emerging out of the collapse of communism, ones which I would find exciting. There seemed, for example, the possibility of new kinds of feminisms and approaches to gender relations. In fact, the whole field of gender studies has taken off since then, with courses having been introduced in universities, exchange schemes organised and so on. Hostility to feminism is no longer universal, and the exhaustion with ideology that I described in the immediate post-communist period seems to have passed away. Nevertheless, I don't think that things have necessarily got better for women. Women have drawn upon their extraordinary resourcefulness to survive and even in some cases prosper. However, gender is still not part of the discussions of transformation and/or transition. Since that time I have been conducting interviews and surveys in a range of post-communist countries and have a better sense of the life of ordinary people rather than the sparkling young elite that I met at the Central European University.

In the Central European countries and those drawn into the orbit of the European Union, we are seeing societies very much like western European ones emerging. In those countries destroyed by civil war, external aggression and by sanctions, many of the achievements of civilisation over the last fifty years have been lost. In many countries of the former Soviet Union, families are thrown back on their own resources to survive and women's activities are absolutely crucial in this. It is their daily efforts under very difficult and uncertain conditions that enable social and economic life to continue at all. It is their work in maintaining the social cohesion of families and informal networks that enables other family members to conduct their lives with less hardship. All in all, we must take a much more mixed view of the transformation from communism than we did in the early 1990s. It has been neither as quick nor as positive as we initially expected. After a decade of transition, most people in the post-communist countries are worse off than they were under communism. This is especially the case when we move away from the charmed belt of successful transition countries on the borders of Europe - Poland, Hungary, the Czech Republic and Slovenia - and further to the East and the South. For many households in these regions, capitalism has brought a radical de-modernisation instead of the modernisation they had hoped for, as a large proportion rely more than ever on their garden plots or the informal economy to survive. Social security and income from the formal economy have both dried up. In a recent survey of young women in Bulgaria, for example, we found that two thirds of those under 30 were without any income at all. At the same time, flashy consumerism is visible in the new cafes, cars and plastic chairs parked around the cities, evidence of selective prosperity and some real diversity in living conditions.

Older women who sacrificed their youth to building a brave new society, and their prime years in shouldering the 'double burden', now stand shamefully at the side of the road trying to sell small artefacts and comestibles. Or dig potatoes to feed their children and grandchildren in the city. Some, of course, have escaped or found better ways to earn a living, but this is not a real possibility for the majority of older women. They are the real victims of transition. They see little of the benefits of transition, which have gone mainly to a younger, more selfish, more mobile and more educated generation. Hence, many older women look back on the communist period with nostalgia and vote for those leaders who promise to restore some of the lost security from that era.

One of the achievements of communism was the raising of universal educational standards, especially for women, who had higher educational standing there than in western Europe. Many of these women are now dequalified as they are no longer able to use their qualifications in the labour market, or they find that the more traditionally qualified jobs in the feminised sectors of the labour market (teaching, medicine) are very poorly rewarded. Nevertheless, education is still an important source of social mobility.

We see different groups of women with very different and diverging prospects. Globalisation brings new media, new forms of communication and new economic prospects for some, while bringing degrading conditions for others.

Furthermore, the women's issues which have surfaced into public life, such as concern about the trafficking of women for sexual purposes, have not really helped the majority of women. Although this kind of criminal exploitation is clearly serious, it tends to present Eastern European women as victims to be 'saved'. Once more, the western missionaries have found a cause to champion. The explosion of prostitution since the opening of the Eastern borders of Europe is something that deserves some serious attention, but it should be perhaps seen more in terms of the survival strategies pursued by women when other possibilities for earning a living are drying up. The many more mundane and humiliating tasks done by women to help ensure the well-being of their families should also be subject to investigation. Much of this day-to-day invisible work of women has helped to ensure that the transition from communism has not resulted in much worse hardship.

Furthermore, we need not even see all this as 'transition' any more. It is simply the real conditions of life and may not improve, or only very slowly. Although there is widespread optimism that a better world is still just round the corner (even if it is further off than they originally anticipated), it is unlikely to arrive in time to help many of the women on whose backs both the old world and the new world were built.

I am grateful to Siyka Kovatcheva for her comments and intellectual support.

This article was first published in 1995. It is published here in English for the first time, with a new afterword.

Silesian Lutherans

A Polish religious minority with a confused history in the borderlands of Central Europe

Photoessay by Grazyna Kubica-Heller

Grazyna Kubica-Heller works as a social anthropologist at Jagiellonian University, Krakow. Her main interests are the study of religious minorities and the symbolic dimension of culture. This photo essay is a representation of her encounter with the Protestant minority in Catholic Poland. After Poland's return to civil society, a successful transition will also be measured by the ways in which the newly created civil society will deal with, and allow space for, its own minorities, such as the Lutherans.

Right: *Their faces as gentle and easy as the mountains around.*

Left: Was the sense of guilt stronger in her or was it the grace of faith, the inevitability of punishment or the certainty of salvation, conviction about the power of sin or the hope of exculpation. These Lutheran dilemmas had also to be present within her.

Above: A grey crowd is pouring out of the church. People are working their ways through the rain, wind and cold of the world. People warmed up in their devotion, their faith and grace are returning to the cold of their houses.

There was the whole family going to the place 'by the stone' under the leadership of the grandmother. All were wearing comfortable shoes, all were carrying bottles of water and sandwiches in their rucksacks, only the presence of hymn-books inside them made the event different from an ordinary Sunday trip to the mountains.

She died just before Easter, or rather sufficiently before, so as not to add to anybody's trouble by her leave, not to interrupt preparations, not to disturb Lenten confusion - disarray before Easter.

Of her three brothers, only Ernest survived the war – kept as a Polish officer in a German flag, Jan died for being a Pole in a concentration camp, while Carol was killed as a Wehrmacht soldier in Yugoslavia, who knows by whom.

Dress rehearsal

Ends or means? Problems of republican discourse in contemporary Britain

Interview with Jonathan Freedland

Andreas Hess *talks to Guardian columnist* Jonathan Freedland.

Recently Anthony Hopkins's application for American citizenship caused an outcry in his hometown Port Talbot and in Wales. Why do you think people were so upset?

It shows you that people in Britain are still sensitive. They don't like the idea that somehow their country might be inferior to America. They were under the impression that in Anthony Hopkins's case the sentimental and blood attachment was now topped by the lavish riches of being an American citizen. Everyone knows that's true, but for him to say it publicly was such a profound gesture, a gesture that has depressed people.

So Britain is a jealous nation?

There's no doubt about that. I think a psychologist would really have a field day if Britain was on the couch discussing its relationship with America. Jealousy is definitely a part of it, and a kind of sibling rivalry. Britain feels that it has something in common with America, that we should be the same, we've both got the English language - and yet somehow they're doing better than us. Or, that Britain is the kind of older sister that stayed at home to look after the parent, and that America is the young reckless kid, the son who went out to make his fortune in the world. Now he insists on coming back to visit, showing off the fast car he's got parked outside and the glamorous girlfriend he's brought back from California. And the dowdy English spinster is at home thinking, that could have been me. So that's part of it. But, to pick a different family relationship, there's also a very deep feeling that we are the parent of America, in the sense that we started it.

Greece to their Rome?

Greece to their Rome, and the Motherland and Fatherland. The old country is all of those things; and somewhere in that relationship is the kind of envy that Laius felt towards Oedipus: here is my son who is going to outgrow and ultimately topple and replace me. Britain feels that about America. We were the Empire, and we spawned this new young infant and upstart who has dared to outstrip the parent. It's like a parental relationship in that there is a combination of envy and also some degree of kinship and even pride, so that we are drawn to America, even as we feel smaller because of it. It's such a complicated relationship psychologically. In the book *Bring Home the Revolution* I talk about Greece to their Rome, but I also talk about Alfred to their Batman, which I feel is a slightly more popular culture expression of the same thing. Alfred is weak and old and decrepit, while Bruce Wayne is rich and fit, strong and more attractive. But in the end Alfred feels he's really the smart one, he's the one with the brain power, he's the wise counsel restraining the hot-headed youngster, he's the Greece to Bruce Wayne's Rome - exactly how Harold Macmillan and Harold Wilson used to imagine themselves in relationship to America. So I just think if you were Anthony Clare or Oliver James and you had Britain walk in as your patient, wanting to talk about its relationship with America, you'd think, 'This is going to be a very rich vein'.

With reference to the political-cultural relationship between America and Britain, maybe we could start with the 'republican checklist' at the end of your book? It included such points as popular sovereignty, more democracy, a new republic, separation of power, guaranteed rights and a constitution ... If you think about that sort of checklist, how does the Blair government score in this?

The thread of logic that goes through those ten steps to the revolution is in a way captured by those two words 'popular sovereignty'. The common theme is the notion of the people being in charge. If the people are in charge, they should choose their own head of state - so you arrive at the demand for a republic. If the people are in charge, that means they own their own country, they should have an owner's manual - which is what, after all, a written constitution amounts to. If the people are in charge, they have a right to see the documents explaining the decisions taken in their name - so you'd have a freedom of information act. If the people are in charge, they should choose their own law-makers - that means an elected second chamber, not an appointed or hereditary one. So, the theme is the people being in charge. Judged by that thread, it's certainly not an avowed aim of this government; the government does not use that rhetoric. They don't say 'the one defining theme of our project is that where people are currently not in charge of their own lives, they now should be'. I happen to think they could use that rhetoric and it would be very effective if they did, but they don't. So, when you judge them by that test, you're judging them by a test they did not set for themselves. On that measure, the answer is boringly mixed. On the one hand they have put the people more in charge of their lives than they were before: the Scots and the Welsh get to choose the people who spend their public money; Londoners get to choose the mayor; there's going to be a slightly better freedom of information act. Those are just a few obvious changes where people are now more in charge. On the other hand, you have to look at what they're doing in education or in health - education being the most outrageous example. Previously, local education authorities gave a measure of local democracy in education-spending decisions, but they are about to be bypassed in Gordon Brown's budget of this year. The money will now go directly to head-teachers. The government says that this is the ultimate devolution - down to head-teacher level, but the Tories said the same about what they were doing with economic decentralisation and it wasn't true. In the area of health

Labour is ever more centralising. I know that Tony Blair privately says, in referring to the health sector, that we have to centralise in order to decentralise. But that is reminiscent of the old Vietnam line, 'we have to bomb the village in order to save it'. That's where they are, and the public can see the contradiction - not least in all these examples of control-freakery in elections in Wales and London, with Rhodri Morgan and Ken Livingstone. Labour says that they are giving power to the people, and in some areas that's true - but they're acting in the opposite way in others.

Don't you think that this contradiction can be explained by the fact that these people have been brought up with a tradition of parliamentary sovereignty and supremacy. They have been socialised in certain ways ...

Oh yes, I wasn't addressing myself here particularly to explanations. I think you're absolutely right, you can't expect creatures of a system to change that system. They are products and creatures of the Westminster system and therefore of a highly centralised British state. So that's what they know. It's almost an eternal truth that people may complain about excesses of centralised power when they don't have it, but when they get it they begin suddenly to see merits that they hadn't previously noticed! For example, opposition parties, once they arrive in office, have always found that freedom of information reduces executive power. Even now the Tories are talking about giving more strength to the freedom of information act. They won't talk that way when they're in power again. Clearly, since 2 May 1997 Labour has had power and they've got used to it. No minister wants to act to the contrary, by giving away some of their own power.

The other point is more an intellectual argument about the left. The left has always been interested in ends rather than means, and I think they think that efficiency of outcome is jeopardised - or at least not helped particularly - by democracy of means. Take education: they just think we want the schools to be better, therefore we've got to take charge of them, because we'll grab them by the scruff of the neck and we'll sort them out - 'I'll do it right here, from behind my desk'. That's the thinking. 'I am doing the right thing, I am Gordon Brown, I know what to do'. I think the intentions are good, they want the schools to be better. But what they don't think is: 'I want the schools to be better, therefore I'm going to put them in the hands of people chosen by those who live close to and work in and use those schools'. They think democracy, if anything, is an actual impediment to an efficient outcome, a sort of encumbrance: it's going to delay, it's going to be messy, it's going to take months to get it right. They certainly don't see it as the route to better outcomes. And that's the thing about the left, they've always favoured outcomes above all. They're not interested in the process.

Can we talk a little bit more about the problem of where change could come from? When you've being socialised in certain ways, where will change come from if not from long-term perspectives, the furtherance of citizenship education?

I think the people agitating for change tend to be people who have had experiences elsewhere. There's lots and lots of people who have seen other places in the world working well, and you have now a sort of political core who've had experiences, particularly, in the United States. William Hague, even though he is a Eurosceptic, went to Insead, the French-based business school. All the people around Brown seem to come out of Harvard. The Downing Street policy unit consists of Kennedy and Harvard scholars. They know from experience about the world outside. Previous governing classes of this country also probably had lived outside, in the world, but two things are different. The first thing is there isn't now the kind of arrogant belief, as there might have been in the 1940s or 1950s, that the British system is perfect and it's the best. Back then, if you went abroad, your job was to tell other countries how good Britain was and how they might possibly have a stab at becoming like Britain. It's a sort of institutional hooliganism, where you go around saying 'you must have the Westminster-style parliament'. There has definitely been a change in that. The other thing is that globalisation has made a big change; now one is exposed to other systems and other ways of governing all the time. More knowledge and information about these things is available - to such an extent that some teenager in Downing Street is now able to read the *New York Times* on-line in the morning. I think we are all now exposed to a different set of influences, and that goes hand in hand with a kind of erosion of the super-confident arrogance about the British system. As for the future, I don't know. When you say citizenship education, I think that's putting the cart before the horse. There has to be the demand to be citizens, and an understanding of what that is, before, as a society, we are going to commit ourselves to teaching the next generation and teaching our children as if they were citizens. I think the demand for that is coming from the roots. It's bubbling up in a way which is not obviously political, but which is actually more cultural. There is something in the pop culture which has been loosely branded by this 'end of deference' tag. There's something going on among younger people. Instead of being passive and subject-like, they're now being active and more demanding, as consumers. I remain a bit optimistic that at the most trashy, street, level you're beginning to see that kind of thing fed through - like the girl-power thing that happened in the mid-1990s among teenage girls. And I notice it, for example, in the tone of emails and letters I get in response to my columns in the *Guardian*. When they're from younger readers, there is a definite sense of empowerment about them. There's an assumption that they have absolutely every right to hold very strong opinions and that they don't have to take advice from anyone. They are absolutely active, empowered and they are - they wouldn't use the word, but I do - citizens. I'm quite encouraged by that and I think that's come from many broader swirls in the culture. It's those indications rather than obviously political ones that indicate change.

Can we move on a little bit from culture to politics? One thing to be learned from the US experience would definitely be to have a more coherent approach - the keyword here is federalism - and not just the little bits and pieces that are given away 'from above'. Devolution, as the name implies, is from above: Scotland has been a little bit more lucky than Wales, and we can continue to debate about how much power the London mayor actually has. So what about a more coherent approach?

First, on the point about devolution, you're completely right, except I think that the point about the word is not necessarily about power flowing from above but from the centre. That's how I see the word work, that there is this huge power which belongs at the centre until something's devolved outward, spun outward. It's a circular image rather than a vertical one. But the point is exactly right; devolution assumes a kind of archaic structure in the first place.

As for coherence, well, the immediate answer to that is about Britain and tradition. We are a messy political culture and that's held to be part of the charm of our system: it's messy and patchy; we just piece-meal things together. To quote Andrew Sullivan, this is the British mentality: 'not for us Teutonic coherence and Gallic uniformity'. On the Continent they've always gone in for neat systems. This is, as I understand it, the difference between English and Continental philosophy. They prefer neat and ordered systems where we have always been more pragmatic and empirical. That has translated even now into a kind of 'what-works' system, where we just patch things up and put them together. That's the traditional response to that question. But I would say that there's a bit more to it than that. When you look at the way Britain is governed, it's partly governed with smoke and mirrors. You know Bagehot reflects this very well; effectively, the whole way the British constitution is structured is to pull wool over the eyes of the great uneducated masses who aren't fit to make political decisions. That's how Bagehot writes, admittedly satirically, but that's what he's saying, that we have to construct all these ways to conceal from the British people the truth of their own system. Therefore the more you begin to write it down and order it, the more people would immediately say 'what on earth is the logic of this?'. If you actually wrote a written constitution as a description of what Britain is now like, everyone would just look at it and think 'this is mad', having all this power in the hands of the executive. Look at how many chunks of it are totally unelected and undemocratic. So, instead, it's actually better from the rulers' point of view if it's incoherent and messy, with lots of traditions and conventions, because that means there's something to hide behind. That way people don't ever really get a good hard look at it. I think that's the whole point of why in Britain there are these rituals and elaborate royal titles. The State Opening of Parliament is deliberately a ritual that nobody could possibly understand, with 'the Silverstick in waiting', and the first Lord Chamberlain of the Admiralty, or whatever it is, and no-one knows the procedure or understands it. That's a pretty effective strategy for the governing class to make sure that no-one can be let in on the secret of the priesthood. I don't buy into that stuff, but that is just how we do things. It's how the governing class do things, and they do it deliberately to keep people out. Manners are another kind of etiquette where you make rules so that only 'we' will understand them and the people outside can't be included.

Federalism poses some more legitimate concerns. In relation to the first point about coherence, I think people would be put off because they then would have to systematise a set of circumstances that at the moment serves people well by not being systematic. The second merit of the current system is a legitimate one, which relates to the nature of the countries which make up the United Kingdom. One, England, is bigger and more populous than all the others and that creates an immediate imbalance. In fact there is no federal system in the world where one of the federal units has, let's say, 85 per cent of the population as a whole. The only way to create a genuine federalist system in this country would be to effectively break up England for administrative purposes, so that you would have units such as Cornwall, Tyneside or London taking their places in a federal structure alongside Wales, Scotland and Northern Ireland. That way you'd get some equivalence in population terms. I think the English are not prepared for that as yet.

Europe, it seems, complicates these matters even more. Sometimes it appears to me that another solution could be that of being an offshore island like Hong Kong - dealing with large financial matters, with a little bit of devolution, and the rest will be provided and taken care of by the EU.

Britain as the Hong Kong of Europe, that's very interesting in itself. And you may be right, but I'd like to hear the argument for it.

Thinking further about the EU - although not necessarily along 'Hong Kong lines'- is already done by other countries within the union. They say 'we have to go a step further, this is not enough'. It will not be the United States of Europe, but we will be going along that route anyway, and it makes less and less sense to think along the line of separate but equal nation states.

Yes, but if that is an argument for how Britain might be integrated in Europe, why does it have to be like that? Why should Britain internally adopt a more federal structure just to fit with Europe?

What I am getting at is the problem of the nation state. Some political scientists have said that the nation state is too small and too big at the same time. Further decentralisation is necessary so that more local units could interact better. Take the example of Catalonia or Baden Wuerthemberg. These are very powerful regions which already have a strong representative voice in Brussels. These regions will make a case for further decentralisation and empowerment. Germany, for example, is already too big a unit to work in a nimble and agile way at a European level. Even France has de-centralised over the last 15 years.

You say that Loire will negotiate directly in Brussels?

They are doing it already.

There is a neatness to that. That would be certainly the argument of the Scottish National Party. Scotland in Europe, that makes sense, and it would work for Plaid Cymru as well. It would be a neater fit. But just think again about the UK as a whole: just because decentralising and regionalising is what everyone else is doing, it doesn't necessarily mean that there is the same need for us to do that. In other words, I would want Britain to be decentralised, but there's something about what you're saying, the one-size-fits-all kind of thing, that somehow rankles with me a little. If the European project is to work it's got to allow room for some countries to be different - because some countries just have different ways of doing things. I actually would like Britain to go that route, to become more decentralised and federal. I would not have that 'English Problem', with a capital E and a capital P. Nevertheless, my sort of British kick-over-the-statues mentality makes me think 'why do we have to fit better with Europe'?

The answer would be, because equality of conditions is a requirement for a civil society. We have to have some sort of political equality …

So the people of the South West of England should have the same sort of representation as the people of Bavaria for example, if it's to work? Well, that's true and I am, as you know, an admirer of the American federal system. There is an equivalence there between Alabama and Nebraska, even though they are different. Incidentally, during a recent debate with Tom Nairn I started thinking over a potential way of looking at this English problem - I'm not going to say a solution to it. The parallel seems to be either the American South or Scandinavia. People are worried about giving up England in order to go down the federal route, but not because they want England as a political entity (the truth is we don't even have England as a political entity now, it's concealed under the UK system of Westminster). They worry that if we had a federal system, in which Britain would have fifteen constituent parts, it would entail the break-up of England. It's not really the political entity that worries people but losing England as a cultural area. One reason why I mentioned Scandinavia and the American South is that they share a particular feature. There is no political union of the American South; the American South does not send two senators to Washington DC to represent them. The South got broken up. (Actually, it was always broken up, it's Virginia, Alabama, etc.) Similarly you could say that Scandinavia still symbolises a meaningful common content, but they organise themselves politically as Denmark, Sweden, etc. This, it seems to me, is what the English may have to begin to get their heads around. Just as there is an association of Southern States with governors meeting to talk about their shared political interests, you could imagine an association of English regions, provinces or territories, talking about themselves as English and flying the St George's flag and singing 'Jerusalem' at their annual conference. People would say 'I'm English' in exactly the way that a man from Mississippi might say 'I'm a Southerner'. I think that maybe just as you're either Alabaman or Danish when you're voting, you may be Southern or Scandinavian in terms of your cultural living. That may be the way out of this for the English: voting as a Tynesider while still feeling culturally English.

This brings us to the last question. What do you think England or Britain stands for - as opposed to, for example, the USA?

As for the American side, I still think popular sovereignty is the goal there. The goal of the founding Americans was to find the one place in the world where the people could govern themselves. And when that idea came it didn't exist anywhere else in the world. It has always leant more heavily on the constitution than the Declaration of Independence.

I want to loudly applaud your question because that's what I think the British debate absolutely has to address - not 'Cool Britannia', not 'After Britain' and 'The Day Britain Died' or 'The Abolition of Britain' but 'what is Britain for?' That is exactly the question. All these discussions about saving Britain and constitutional reform are useless unless you have an idea of what it's for. America challenges other countries because America's for something. You and I could debate what it's for, but it's clearly for something; but Britain hasn't been and now it must be. Britain used to be for empire, but now I think we have to invent a new purpose. My answer would be that we live in a hugely diverse world, ethnically, but that these islands are more historically diverse than people realise. When we ask 'what is Britain for?', we have to think what the alternative is. Is it to break off just into England, Scotland and Wales? Those nations do not have, on their own, a record of diversity and multi-ethnicity; it's not written into their very concept. But those ideas are written into the very concept of Britain, because Britain was the first multi-national state, made up of four nations. We're used to the idea of difference being contained within the whole; I think it may have been one of the things we gave to the founding, settler nations of North America. We understood the idea that you can create something out of several other somethings, you can weld them together and still keep the difference. Therefore, we're in the habit of national diversity and can, in turn, be in the habit of ethnic diversity. I can call myself a Jewish Briton or a British Jew; Gary Younge can call himself a black Briton. Neither of us probably would feel comfortable with the label 'English'; that would not trip off my tongue, and my guess is that Gary would not call himself a 'black Englishman'; he would say it estranged him. Yet Britain is a word that we can both embrace because it contains and accepts others in its very concept, and we have to cling on to it. And we're strong when we're strung together.

If you were proposing that in terms of football teams, what would you say?

I wouldn't be averse to a UK football team, but I'm not a huge football fan so I may not be the best judge. I understand that people have historical identities and that the individual, national, teams of England, Scotland and Wales have built up huge identities, and certainly passions, all their own. Just as we accept being decentralised or devolved, that it's right that we have a Scottish Parliament or a Welsh Assembly, you've obviously got to think about devolved football teams. People want them and we shouldn't underestimate their history. I learned recently that the very first international football fixture was England against Scotland in 1872. So therefore these things have real roots which you can't wave aside. What might be nice to say, on my model, is that there is an English and Scottish and Welsh team - and then there is also a UK team for other competitions. Maybe we should be able to flow between the two just as I would like at some point to have a UK parliament in Westminster, sometimes a regional assembly in Cornwall and then sometimes a European parliament in Strasbourg. You can have lots of levels in football communities. Why not one day eventually have a European football team to challenge the Americas: that would be a good tournament. Mind you, I don't know though how many English players would be in it.

The Socialist Project

Revisiting *The Red Paper on Scotland*

Owen Dudley Edwards   **Larry Elliott**
Tom Nairn   **Doreen Massey**
Neal Ascherson   **Bob Jessop**
Sheila Rowbotham   **Hilary Wainwright**

Socialist theory and practice 25 years after Gordon Brown's seminal book

A one-day conference on Friday 1st December 2000

Kings College, University of Aberdeen

John McAllion MP MSP, Labour
Kenny McAskill MSP, Scottish National Party
Tommy Sheridan MSP, Scottish Socialist Party
Susan Deacon MSP, Labour
Minister for Health, Scottish Executive
Chairs: **Lesley Riddoch and Tom Devine**

Registration: £25 including buffet supper; £12.50 student/ unwaged
Cheques payable to University of Aberdeen
Contact: Fraser MacDonald and Andy Cumbers
Arkleton Centre, St Mary's, King's College, Aberdeeen AB24 3UF,
Tel: 01224 273901 Fax: 01224 273902 Email: ark040@abdn.ac.uk
http://www.abdn.ac.uk/arkleton/redpaper

Sponsored by the Barry Amiel and Norman Melburn Trust
Hosted by the Arkleton Centre for Rural Development Research and the
Department of Geography, University of Aberdeen

American Social and
Political Thought
A Concise Introduction

by Andreas Hess
Lecturer in Sociology at the
University of Wales, Bangor

Paperback   160pp   0 7486 1228 9
£12.95 Edinburgh University Press

This is a concise but comprehensive introduction to modern American social and political thought. The author aims to demonstrate the rich intellectual tradition of the United States and to facilitate a better understanding of American society and politics through careful exploration of key social and political theories and theorists.

In the first half of the book the author focuses on introducing the core traditions of American social and political thought - Exceptionalism, Protestantism, Republicanism, Liberalism and Pragmatism. The second half applies these traditions to a broad range of twentieth-century conditions and issues - Power and Democracy, Justice and Injustice, Multiculturalism and Pluralism, Civil Society, Social Theory and Intellectuals. The works of some of the most influential figures in the field, such as de Tocqueville, Lipset, Arendt, Hartz, Pocock, Dewey, Moore, Rawls, Walzer, Rorty and Alexander, are drawn upon to illustrate the theories and issues being discussed.

Order from Edinburgh University Press
22 George Square, Edinburgh EH8 9LF
Tel 0131 650 4220   Fax 0131 662 0053
Email: marketing@eup.ed.ac.uk
Visit our website at www.eup.ed.ac.uk

Soundings back issues

Issue 1 – Launch Issue – Stuart Hall on New Labour / Beatrix Campbell on communitarianism / Fred Halliday on the international order / Mae-Wan Ho on genetic engineering / Barbara Castle on Labour / Simon Edge on gay politics.

Issue 2 – Law & Justice, edited by Bill Bowring – contributors – Kate Markus, Keir Starmer, Ken Wiwa, Kader Asmal, Mike Mansfield, Jonathan Cooper, Ethan Raup, John Griffith, Keith Ewing, Ruth Lister and Anna Coote. Plus Steven Rose on neurogenetic determinism / Jeffrey Weeks on sexual communities / David Bell on Dennis Potter.

Issue 3 – Heroes & Heroines – contributors – Barbara Taylor, Jonathan Rutherford, Graham Dawson, Becky Hall, Anna Grimshaw, Simon Edge, Kirsten Notten, Susannah Radstone, Graham Martin and Cynthia Cockburn. Plus Anthony Barnett on Di's Divorce / David Donnison on New Labour / John Gill and Nick Hallam on Euro '96.

Issue 4 – The Public Good – edited by Maureen Mackintosh – contributors – Gail Lewis, Francie Lund, Pam Smith, Loretta Loach, John Clarke, Jane Falkingham, Paul Johnson, Will Hutton, Charlie King, Anne Simpson, Brigid Benson, Candy Stokes, Anne Showstack Sassoon, Sarabajaya Kumar, Ann Hudock, Carlo Borzaga and John Stewart. Plus Paul Hirst and Grahame Thompson on globalisation / Anne Phillips on socialism and equality / Richard Levins on critical science.

Issue 5 – (out of print) Media Worlds – edited by Bill Schwarz and David Morley – contributors – James Curran, Sarah Benton, Esther Leslie, Angela McRobbie, David Hesmondhalgh, Jonathan Burston, Kevin Robins, Tony Dowmunt and Tim O'Sullivan. Plus Phil Cohen on community / Duncan Green on Latin America / Cynthia Cockburn on women in Israel.

Issue 6 – (out of print) 'Young Britain' – edited by Jonathan Rutherford – contributors – Jonathan Keane, Bilkis Malek, Elaine Pennicott, Ian Brinkley, John Healey, Frances O'Grady, Rupa Huq, Michael Kenny and Peter Gartside. Plus Miriam Glucksmann on Berlin Memories / Costis Hadjimichalis on Europe / Joanna Moncrieff on psychiatric imperialism.

Issue 7 – States of Africa – edited by Victoria Brittain and Rakiya Omaar – contributors – Basil Davidson, Augustin Ndahimana Buranga, Kathurima M'Inoti, Lucy Hannan, Jenny Matthews, Ngugi Wa Mirii, Kevin Watkins, Joseph Hanlon, Laurence Cockcroft, Joseph Warioba, Vic Allen and James Motlasi. Plus Bill Schwarz on the Conservatives / Wendy Wheeler on 'uncanny families' / Dave Featherstone on 'Pure Genius'.

Issue 8 – Active Welfare – edited by Andrew Cooper – contributors – Rachel Hetherington and Helen Morgan John Pitts, Angela Leopold, Hassan Ezzedine, Alain Grevot, Margherita Gobbi, Angelo Cassin and Monica Savio. Plus Michael Rustin on higher education / Colette Harris on Tajikistan / Patrick Wright interview.

Issue 9 – **European Left** – edited by Martin Peterson – contributors – Branka Likic-Brboric, Mate Szabo, Leonadis Donskis, Peter Weinreich, Alain Caille, John Crowley, Ove Sernhede and Alexandra Alund. Plus Angela McRobbie on the music industry / Mario Petrucci on responsibility for future generations / Philip Arestis and Malcolm Sawyer on the new monetarism.

Issue 10 – **Windrush Echoes** – edited by Gail Lewis and Lola Young – contributors – Anne Phoenix, Jackie Kay, Julia Sudbury, Femi Franklin, David Sibley, Mike Phillips, Phil Cole, Bilkis Malek, Sonia Boyce, Roshi Naidoo, Val Wilmer and Stuart Hall. Plus Alan Finlayson on Labour and modernisation / Richard Moncrieff on the Ivory Coast / Mario Pianta on Italy.

Issue 11 – **Emotional Labour** – edited by Pam Smith – contributors – Stephen Lloyd Smith, Dympna Casey, Marjorie Mayo, Minoo Moallem, Prue Chamberlayne, Rosy Martin, Sue Williams and Gillian Clarke. Plus Andreas Hess on individualism and identity/ T. V. Sathyamurthy on South Asia / Les Black, Tim Crabbe and John Solomos on 'Reggae Boyz'.

Issue 12 – **Transversal Politics** – edited by Cynthia Cockburn and Lynette Hunter – contributors – Nira Yuval-Davis, Pragna Patel, Marie Mulholland, Rebecca O'Rourke, Gerri Moriarty, Jane Plastow and Rosie. Plus Bruno Latour on the Left / Gerry Hassan on Scotland / Nick Jeffrey on racism in South East London.

Issue 13 – **These Sporting Times** – edited by Andrew Blake – contributors – Carol Smith, Simon Cook, Adam Brown, Steve Greenfield, Guy Osborne, Gemma Bryden, Steve Hawes, Alan Tomlinson and Adam Locks. Plus Geoff Andrews on New Labour / Fred Halliday on Turkey / Nick Henry and Adrian Passmore on Birmingham.

Issue 14 – **One-Dimensional Politics** – edited by Wendy Wheeler and Michael Rustin – contributors – Wendy Wheeler, Michael Rustin, Dave Byrne, Gavin Poynter, Barry Richards and Mario Petrucci. Plus Ann Briggs on Bullying / David Renton on South Africa / Isaac Balbus on the 1960s/ Laura Dubinsky on US trade unions.

Issue 15 – **States of Mind** – edited by Michael Rustin – contributors – Alan Shuttleworth, Andrew Cooper, Helen Lucey, Diane Reay, Richard Graham and Jennifer Wakelyn. Plus Nancy Fraser on the left/ Stephen Wilkinson on Cuba/ Mike Waite on social entrepreneurs/ Kate Young on violence against women in Bangladesh.

Soundings book – **The Next Ten Years** – Sarah Benton on people and government/ Anthony Barnett on constitutional reform/ Mary Hickman on Northern Ireland/ Ash Amin on regional inequality/ Jean Gardner on women / Tim Lang on food/ Kerry Hamilton and Susan Hoyle on transport/ Bill Bowring on law and order/ Gavi Poynter on unions/ Richard Wilkinson on health

All back issues cost £9.99, post-free. *The Next Ten Years* costs £7.99, post-free.

Send your orders to Soundings, Lawrence and Wishart, 99a Wallis Road, London E9 5LN.
Or email to soundings@l-w-bks.demon.co.uk. Tel 020 8533 2506 Fax 020 8533 7369

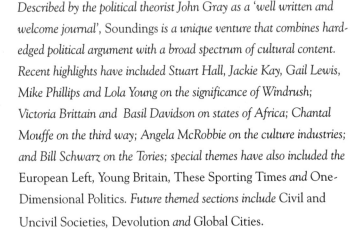

Described by the political theorist John Gray as a 'well written and welcome journal', Soundings is a unique venture that combines hard-edged political argument with a broad spectrum of cultural content. Recent highlights have included Stuart Hall, Jackie Kay, Gail Lewis, Mike Phillips and *Lola Young on the significance of Windrush; Victoria Brittain and Basil Davidson on states of Africa; Chantal Mouffe on the third way; Angela McRobbie on the culture industries;* and *Bill Schwarz on the Tories; special themes have also included the* European Left, Young Britain, These Sporting Times *and* One-Dimensional Politics. *Future themed sections include* Civil and Uncivil Societies, Devolution *and* Global Cities.

SPECIAL OFFER TO NEW SUBSCRIBERS

First time individual subscribers are entitled to a
£25 subscription for the first year

Subscription rates 2001 (3 issues)

Individual subscriptions: *UK* £35.00   *Rest of the World* £45

Institutional subscriptions: *UK* £70.00   *Rest of the World* £80.00

To subscribe, send your name and address and payment (cheque or credit card), stating which issue you want the subscription to start with, to Soundings, Lawrence and Wishart, 99a Wallis Road, London E9 5LN.

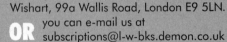 you can e-mail us at
OR subscriptions@l-w-bks.demon.co.uk